Books written by Jack Hartman

Trust God for Your Finances 1983 (over 175,000 copies in print)
Nuggets of Faith 1984
One Hundred Years from Today 1985
How to Study the Bible 1985
Never, Never Give Up 1994
Quiet Confidence in the Lord 1996

Books co-authored with Judy Hartman

Increased Energy and Vitality 1994
God's Wisdom Is Available to You 2001
Exchange Your Worries for God's Perfect Peace 2003
Unshakable Faith in Almighty God 2004
Receive Healing from the Lord 2006
What Does God Say? 2008
Victory Over Adversity 2009
God's Joy Regardless of Circumstances 2009
A Close and Intimate Relationship with God 2010
Overcoming Fear 2011
Effective Prayer 2011
God's Instructions for Growing Older 2012
You Can Hear the Voice of God 2012
God's Plan for Your Life 2013
Reverent Awe of God 2013
Glorious Eternal Life in Heaven 2014
Live Continually in the Presence of God 2014

Scripture Meditation Cards with accompanying CDs (1996-2000) co-authored by Jack and Judy Hartman

A Closer Relationship with the Lord
Continually Increasing Faith in God
Enjoy God's Wonderful Peace
Financial Instructions from God
Find God's Will for Your Life
Freedom from Worry and Fear
God Is Always with You
Our Father's Wonderful Love
Receive God's Blessings in Adversity
Receive Healing from the Lord

Live Continually in the Presence of God

Jack and Judy Hartman

**Lamplight Ministries, Inc.,
Dunedin, Florida**

We are excited that you have chosen to read this book. Our prayer is that you will be gripped by God Himself through the Scripture that is contained in this book. We pray that God will speak to your heart and that you will meditate often on these great scriptural truths pertaining to living in the presence of God. Our goal is to help you know God more intimately and to live continually in His presence.

Please visit our website at www.lamplight.net. Please tell us if this book has made a difference in your life. We would like to hear from you. Please send us an email at lamplightmin@yahoo.com or drop us a note at Lamplight Ministries, Inc., P.O. Box 1307, Dunedin, FL, 34697.

Follow us at facebook.com/jackandjudylamplight; blog: lamplightmin@wordpress.com; ebooks: go to SmashWords.com. Type in "Jack Hartman."

You also can request our free monthly newsletter by mail or email. We would like to stay in touch with you with our newsletter. You can see updates on forthcoming books and pray for us as we pray for you. You also can receive a daily devotional from a set of our

Scripture Meditation Cards. You can download the first chapter of each of our books.

Our books that have been translated into other languages are downloadable for free as well. Our mission is to help you get into the Word of God and to help you get the Word of God into yourself.

Copyright 2014

Jack and Judy Hartman

No part of this book may be used or reproduced in any manner whatsoever without written permission from the publisher except in the case of brief quotations and articles of review. For more information regarding this book please contact:

Jack and Judy Hartman
Lamplight Ministries Inc.
PO Box 1307
Dunedin, Florida 34697-2921
Telephone: 1-800-540-1597

FAX: 1-727-784-2980
Website: lamplight.net
Email: lamplightmin@yahoo.com
Facebook: facebook.com/jackandjudylamplight
Twitter: twitter.com/lamplightmin
Blog: lamplightmin.wordpress.com
Ebooks: SmashWords.com. Type in "Jack Hartman"
ISBN: 978-0-915445-57-8
Library of Congress Control Number: 2014921204

Dedication

With deep joy we dedicate this book to Ed Hiers. Neither Jack nor Ed knew what God had in store for both of them when Jack recruited Ed to a sales position in his insurance agency when Ed was 22. Jack made Ed his assistant at the age of 25 and his partner at the age of 28.

The working together of these two men has been a modern day David and Jonathan/father and son relationship. Today Ed is the father of four children and the grandfather of eight grandchildren. He remains at the helm of Northeast Planning Associates, (website: northeastplanning.com), operating this company on biblical principles resulting in extraordinary excellence. Ed also serves as pastor of Shiloh Community Church (website: shilohweb.org) in Manchester, New Hampshire.

Ed, we are in awe of how you pour yourself out like oil to your precious family, the advisors at NPA and your flock at Shiloh. Your father's and your pastor's heart bless everyone around you. Your family, NPA and Shiloh are the results of a life completely surrendered to Jesus Christ. We bless you and love you, Ed, in Jesus' name. Amen.

Table of Contents

Introduction 11
1. God Wants You to Live Continually in His Presence 15
2. Jesus Christ Enables You to Live in the Presence of God 21
3. A Reverent and Intimate Relationship with God ... 27
4. Receive Supernatural Protection by Living in God's Presence 33
5. Pride Can Keep You Out of the Presence of God 39
6. Surrender Control of Your Life 45
7. Only Grateful Christians Live in God's Presence .. 49
8. Thank God Continually 57
9. Praise God Continually 65
10. Sing Praise to God Continually............................. 73
11. Sing Praise to God When You Face Adversity 77
12. An Effective Way to Sing Praise to God 83
13. Recommended Praise and Worship DVDs 89
14. Are You Living in the Presence of God?................ 97
Conclusion 103
Appendix: Trusting in Jesus Christ as Your Savior 107

Introduction

The magnitude of the topic of this book is almost impossible to describe with the limitations of our human understanding. You will see in the upcoming pages that the same God Who created the entire universe wants *you* to live continually in His presence throughout your life on earth.

Everyone in heaven lives continually in the presence of God. There is no better place for any person on earth to be than in the presence of God. We pray that you will approach this book with an open mind to learn exactly what the Bible says about living in the presence of God during the remainder of your life. "...the spiritual man tries all things [he examines, investigates, inquires into, questions, and discerns all things]..." (I Corinthians 2:15)

Make the quality decision that you will carefully study what God's Book of Instructions, the Bible, has to say about coming into God's presence. Turn completely away from the limitations of your human understanding. God said, "...My thoughts are not your thoughts, neither are your ways My ways, says the Lord. For as the heavens are higher than the earth, so are My ways higher than your ways and My thoughts than your thoughts." (Isaiah 55:8-9)

We have spent hundreds of hours studying the Bible to learn the great scriptural truths that we will share with you in this book. We believe that God's instructions and promises pertaining to His presence will transform the life of every person who learns and obeys these instructions and believes completely in God's promises.

We now use *The Amplified Bible* exclusively in our books. I (Jack) have been using *The Amplified Bible* since 1975. At that time only *The Amplified New Testament* was available. I bought this version of the Bible when I saw it in a Christian bookstore because of an inscription from Dr. Billy Graham on the cover. Dr. Graham said, "This is the best Study Testament on the market. It is a magnificent translation. I use it constantly."

The Amplified Bible is the result of the study of a group of Bible scholars who spent a total of more than 20,000 hours amplifying the Bible. They believe that traditional word-by-word translation often fails to reveal the shades of meaning that are part of the original Greek, Hebrew and Aramaic biblical texts.

Their amplification of the original text uses brackets for words that clarify the meaning and parentheses for words that contain additional phrases included in the original language. Through this amplification the reader will gain a better understanding of what Hebrew and Greek listeners instinctively understood.

We would like to give you a specific example of why we use *The Amplified Bible* exclusively:

- "I can do all things through Christ which strengtheneth me." (Philippians 4:13, *The King James Version*)
- "I can do all this through him who gives me strength." (Philippians 4:13, *The New International Version*)
- "I have strength for all things in Christ Who empowers me [I am ready for anything and equal to anything through Him Who infuses inner strength into me; I am self-sufficient in Christ's sufficiency]." (Philippians 4:13, *The Amplified Bible*)

Please note the significant amplification of the original Greek in *The Amplified Bible*. If you make the decision to meditate on Philippians 4:13, you will find that there is much more depth of meaning in *The Amplified Bible* version of this verse.

We recommend that you first read through this book completely. Enjoy God's glorious explanation of the privilege of living continually in His presence.

Then read through the book a second time and highlight or underline all Scripture references and our explanation of this Scripture that is especially meaningful to you. Write notes in the margin or at the top or bottom of each page. If you do, you then will be able to *meditate* on the meaningful passages of Scripture that you have identified as being important to you (see Joshua 1:8 and Psalm 1:2-3).

I (Jack) want to explain why I use the first person on some occasions in our books. I write the first two drafts of each book. Judy then adds her valuable input to the next two drafts. I then write the final two drafts.

I do not want to use the words "I (Jack)" every time I use a first-person reference. I will just use the word "I" whenever I make a personal observation during the remainder of this book. Any personal observations from Judy will be clearly identified.

We blend together our explanations of Scripture. We thank God for the high privilege of dividing His Word, each of us bringing different expertise to create a final book for you. Imagine a husband and wife, each with a bedroom/office at home, working together every day with different viewpoints that God brings together harmoniously. We are very grateful that God has used us in this way since 1991.

We explain each passage of Scripture in simple and easy-to-understand language. We pray that the scriptural contents of this book and our explanation of this Scripture will help you to learn valuable scriptural truths pertaining to the awesome privilege that every child of God has been given to live in God's presence throughout his or her life.

Chapter 1

God Wants You to Live Continually in His Presence

The great truth that *you* have been given the privilege of living in the presence of God throughout your life is overwhelming. Do not make the mistake that many Christians make of knowing little or nothing about what the Bible says regarding God's presence. The apostle Paul explained this spiritual truth to the church in Corinth when he said, "...some of you have not the knowledge of God [you are utterly and willfully and disgracefully ignorant, and continue to be so, lacking the sense of God's presence and all true knowledge of Him]...." (I Corinthians 15:34)

Sadly, unbelievers do not know God's great plan to bring them to Himself and into His presence. Unfortunately, many people who have received Jesus Christ as Savior "are utterly and willfully and disgracefully ignorant" concerning what the Bible says about God's presence.

We have carefully studied God's Word to present the information in this book to you. This book contains more than 180 verses of Scripture that tell you exactly what the Bible says about the presence of God and what God instructs you to do to live continually in His presence. Be like the psalmist who said, "...require His face and His presence [continually] evermore." (Psalm 105:4)

God would not have told you that you can come into His presence and remain there *continually* if you were not able to achieve this goal. There is no better place to be than in the presence of God.

God always emphasizes through repetition. When God tells you the same thing in two or more passages of Scripture, you can be certain that He is emphasizing what He is saying to you. God said, "Seek the Lord and His strength; yearn for and seek His face and to be in His presence continually!" (I Chronicles 16:11)

When you yearn for something, you have a deep desire for whatever you are seeking. As you read this book, we pray that you will yearn to live *continually* in God's presence. The psalmist David said, "You have said, Seek My face [inquire for and require My presence as your vital need]. My heart says to You, Your face (Your presence), Lord, will I seek, inquire for, and require [of necessity and on the authority of Your Word]." (Psalm 27:8)

Please note in the amplification at the beginning of this verse that living in God's presence is "your vital need." Living in God's presence is not a nice-to-have. David was determined to do exactly what the holy Scriptures instructed him to do to live in God's presence. We pray that you will have this same determination in your life. "...the upright shall dwell in Your presence (before Your very face)." (Psalm 140:13)

The word "upright" in this verse refers to your righteousness before God if Jesus Christ is your Savior. When you dwell in a place, you live there permanently. There is no question that God wants you to live continually in His presence. If you are not certain that Jesus Christ is your Savior, please stop reading now and turn to the Appendix at the end of this book. See for yourself exactly what the Word of God instructs you to do to receive Jesus Christ as your Savior.

Please let us know if you have become a member of the family of God. We have free studies and/or downloads for you on our website to keep your faith strong.

We pray that you will understand the enormous magnitude of the privilege that you have been given to live continually in the presence of God. The following verse of Scripture explains the awesomeness of being in the presence of God. "The earth trembled, the heavens also poured down [rain] at the presence of God; yonder Sinai quaked at the presence of God, the God of Israel." (Psalm 68:8)

The psalmist explained that the ability to be in God's presence is so magnificent that the entire earth trembled before the presence of God. Rain poured down from heaven because of the presence of God. An earthquake erupted on Mount Sinai because of the presence of God. "Tremble, O earth, at the presence of the Lord..." (Psalm 114:7)

The privilege of living continually in God's presence is *so* awesome that God instructs you to tremble because *you* have been given the ability to live in His majestic presence throughout the remainder of your life. If Jesus Christ is your Savior, God is your loving Father. "...I will be a Father to you, and you shall be My sons and daughters, says the Lord Almighty." (II Corinthians 6:18)

You have been given the privilege of living continually in God's presence because of your Father's incredible love, grace, compassion and mercy. You have been given this privilege because of the tremendous price that Jesus Christ paid for you when He willingly gave up His life by crucifixion at Calvary and subsequently rose from the dead.

If you learn how to live continually in God's presence, your heart will sing with joy. You will be like the psalmist David who said, "...in Your presence is fullness of joy, at Your right hand there are pleasures forevermore." (Psalm 16:11)

If you learn and obey God's specific instructions telling you how to live continually in His presence, you will experience supernatural joy. The words "fullness of" describe the magnitude of the joy that you will experience if you live continually in God's presence.

Every person in heaven is filled with joy because everyone in heaven lives continually in the presence of God. We pray that you will understand that God has given you the privilege of living continually in His presence while you are here on earth. You do not have to wait until you are in heaven to live continually in the presence of God. "...You will enrapture me [diffusing my soul with joy] with and in Your presence." (Acts 2:28)

The word "enrapture" consists of two parts - "en" and "rapture." The prefix "en" means "in." The word "rapture" means to be carried away with joy. The amplification says that your soul will be diffused with joy. The word "diffused" means to be poured out. God's supernatural joy will be poured into you if you learn and obey His specific instructions to live continually in His magnificent presence. "Humble yourselves [feeling very insignificant] in the presence of the Lord, and He will exalt you [He will lift you up and make your lives significant]." (James 4:10)

If you truly are humble because of the precious privilege that you have been given of living continually in God's presence, your Father will lift you up. He will make your life significant.

We pray that you are in absolute awe of the privilege that you have been given to live continually in God's presence. In the next chapter we will study many Scripture references pertaining to the price that Jesus Christ paid to enable you to live continually in God's presence.

Chapter 2

Jesus Christ Enables You to Live in the Presence of God

We will begin this chapter by studying how Adam and Eve were created to live in the presence of God and how they forfeited this tremendous privilege. God created the Garden of Eden when He created the earth. This place of incredible beauty was where Adam and Eve resided. They were continually in God's presence in this beautiful garden.

God told Adam and Eve that they could eat from every tree in this garden except the tree of the knowledge of good and evil. He told them that they must not eat from this tree and that they surely would die if they did (see Genesis 2:16-17). Adam and Eve disobeyed these specific instructions from God. They ate the forbidden fruit from this tree (see Genesis 3:6).

Adam and Eve died spiritually when they disobeyed God. They severed their ability to live in God's presence. "...they heard the sound of the Lord God walking in the garden in the cool of the day, and Adam and his wife hid themselves from the presence of the Lord God among the trees of the garden." (Genesis 3:8)

This verse explains that Adam and Eve actually hid from the presence of God. All human beings since the fall of Adam have inherited Adam's fallen nature. All human beings come into the world separated from God. In Old Testament times the only way that any human being could come into the presence of God was for a selected high priest to come into God's presence one day each year at the Day of Atonement (see Leviticus Chapters 14, 15 and 16).

This selected high priest coming into the presence of God was a very complicated affair. Moses built a tabernacle following specific instructions from God. This tabernacle consisted of two rooms. The outer room was called the Holy Place. The inner room was called the Holy of Holies. A thick veil was placed between the two rooms to protect the Holy of Holies where the high priest was able to come into the presence of God only one day each year.

When Jesus Christ died on the cross and subsequently rose from the dead, He restored the privilege that Adam forfeited. Jesus made provision for every person to enter into the presence of God.

In His final minute of agony before giving up His life after suffering for approximately three hours on the cross, Jesus made provision for you to come into the presence of God. "...Jesus uttered a loud cry, and breathed out His life. And the curtain [of the Holy of Holies] of the temple was torn in two from top to bottom." (Mark 15:37-38)

When Jesus died on the cross at Calvary, the curtain that separated the Holy Place and the Holy of Holies was destroyed. Coming into God's presence no longer is limited to a high priest being able to come into God's presence one day each year. If Jesus Christ is your Savior, you do not have to go through a priest or anyone else to come directly into the presence of God. "...we have full freedom and confidence to enter into the [Holy of] Holies [by the power and virtue] in the blood of Jesus, by this fresh (new) and living way which He initiated and dedicated and opened for us through the separating curtain (veil of the Holy of Holies), that is, through His flesh" (Hebrews 10:19-20)

If Jesus Christ is your Savior, you have "full freedom" to come into the presence of God. There no longer is a veil blocking you from coming into God's presence. "...now has [Christ, the Messiah] reconciled [you to God] in the body of His flesh through death, in order to present you holy and faultless and irreproachable in His [the Father's] presence." (Colossians 1:22)

When Jesus Christ died on the cross at Calvary, He made it possible for you to once again have the privilege that Adam and Eve enjoyed of living continually in the presence of God. However, you will not enter into the presence of God automatically during your life on earth.

Every Christian will live eternally in the presence of God in heaven. If you want to live in the presence of God during the remainder of your life on earth, you must learn and obey the specific instructions from God that we will explain in the remaining chapters of this book.

Many Christians go to church each week, pray a few moments each day and live a religious lifestyle, but the remainder of their lives is centered around various activities in the world. If Jesus Christ is your Savior, this world is not your home. "...we are citizens of the state (commonwealth, homeland) which is in heaven..." (Philippians 3:20)

You will only enter into the presence of God during your life on earth to the degree that you fully comprehend that the world is not your home. The Bible speaks of Christians as being "...aliens and strangers and exiles [in this world] ..." (I Peter 2:11)

Every person who has received Jesus Christ as his or her Savior is an "alien, stranger and exile" in the world. If you sincerely desire to live in the presence of God, you will consistently turn away from the ways of the world. "Do not be conformed to this world (this age), [fashioned after and adapted to its external, superficial customs]..." (Romans 12:2)

The amplification in this verse speaks of the "external and superficial customs" of the world. You will only be able to live in the presence of God during the remainder of your life on earth to the degree that you "...turn away from the irreverent babble and godless chatter, with the vain and empty and worldly phrases..." (I Timothy 6:20)

See the world as God sees it. The world is filled with irreverent and godless talk. Make the quality decision that you will center every aspect of your life around Jesus Christ, not around anyone or anything in the world. "...He is the Beginning, the Firstborn from among the dead, so that He alone in everything and in every respect might occupy the chief place [stand first and be preeminent]." (Colossians 1:18)

When Jesus Christ rose from the dead, He enabled you to come into God's presence. If you have a deep and sincere desire to live in God's presence, Jesus Christ will "occupy the chief place, stand first and be preeminent" in your life. You will not allow anyone or anything to come ahead of your consistent focus on Jesus Christ Who has earned and deserves the right to be in first place in your life at all times. You will have the same attitude as John the Baptist who said, "He must increase, but I must decrease. [He must grow more prominent; I must grow less so.]" (John 3:30)

The scriptural lifestyle that enables you to come into God's presence requires you to continually increase your focus on Jesus Christ and to decrease your focus on yourself. Jesus wants to be more than your Savior Who will keep you from going to hell. He also wants to be the Lord of every day of your life. "…you must abide in (live in, never depart from) Him [being rooted in Him, knit to Him]…" (I John 2:27)

You are instructed to "abide" in Jesus Christ. The amplification explains that abiding in Jesus Christ is living in Him and never departing from Him. If you truly abide in Christ, your life will be deeply rooted in Him. Every aspect of your life will revolve around Him. You will be like the psalmist who said, "…I have no delight or desire on earth besides You." (Psalm 73:25)

The psalmist's desire was to always put God first in his life. If these words describe your desires, you will be living the way God wants you to live. You will live continually in His presence.

In this chapter we have studied Scripture references that clearly explain how Adam and Eve forfeited the ability to live continually in the presence of God and how Jesus Christ won this privilege back for you. In subsequent chapters we will study many additional passages of Scripture that will thoroughly explain the lifestyle that God wants each of His children to live so that they will come into His presence.

Chapter 3

A Reverent and Intimate Relationship with God

In the last chapter we studied what the Bible says about keeping God first at all times and consistently turning away from the world. In this chapter we will study what the Bible says about the relationship between reverent fear of God, a close and intimate relationship with God and living continually in God's presence.

God created you to fear Him and to obey His instructions. "...Fear God [revere and worship Him, knowing that He is] and keep His commandments, for this is the whole of man [the full, original purpose of his creation, the object of God's providence, the root of character, the foundation of all happiness, the adjustment to all inharmonious circumstances and conditions under the sun] and the whole [duty] for every man." (Ecclesiastes 12:13)

When you fear God, you revere Him. You worship Him continually. Every aspect of your life revolves around Him. The second amplification in this verse says that fearing God and obeying God's instructions are "the purpose for your creation," "the root of character" and "the whole duty for every man."

Doing what God created you to do is vitally important. Your character and all happiness in your life comes from obeying these specific instructions from God. God put reverential fear of Him in your heart when He created you. God said, "...I will put My [reverential] fear in their hearts, so that they will not depart from Me." (Jeremiah 32:40)

Every person is born with the fear of God in his or her heart. God gives each person freedom of choice. You decide throughout your life whether or not you truly will fear God. Many Christians live a religious lifestyle for a few hours each week. Instead of fearing God and revering Him, the remainder of their lives is devoted to doing what they want to do.

If you truly desire to have a close and intimate relationship with God and to live continually in His presence, you will fear God and revere Him continually. "The secret [of the sweet, satisfying companionship] of the Lord have they who fear (revere and worship) Him..." (Psalm 25:14)

Nothing in life is sweeter than a personal relationship with God and living in God's presence. There is no question that a lifestyle of reverential fear of God is essential to living in God's presence. "...you should conduct yourselves with true reverence throughout the time of your temporary residence [on the earth, whether long or short]." (I Peter 1:17)

God instructs you to live a life of reverential fear toward Him throughout your life on earth. Center every day of your life around your reverential fear of God. "...continue in the reverent and worshipful fear of the Lord all the day long." (Proverbs 23:17)

God always emphasizes through repetition. You have seen that your Father has instructed you to fear Him and revere Him throughout your life on earth. We are instructed to "...bring [our] consecration to completeness in the [reverential] fear of God." (II Corinthians 7:1)

The word "consecration" in this context means to devote your life completely to God. If you truly fear God and revere Him, you will live a consecrated life. Every aspect of your life will revolve around God. No worldly activities will come ahead of your reverential fear of God. These words describe the lifestyle that God wants you to live if you sincerely desire to live continually in His presence.

We have studied six Scripture references pertaining to reverential fear of God and living continually in God's presence. We now are ready to study what the Bible teaches about a close and intimate relationship with God and living in His presence. Jesus Christ came into the world so that you can continually draw closer to God. "...the Son of God has [actually] come to this world and has given us understanding and insight [progressively] to perceive (recognize) and come to know better and more clearly Him Who is true — in His Son Jesus Christ (the Messiah). This [Man] is the true God and Life eternal." (I John 5:20)

Your Father wants you to progressively know Him more intimately. He wants the intimacy of your relationship to become deeper with each passing year. "...in

Christ Jesus, you who once were [so] far away, through (by, in) the blood of Christ have been brought near." (Ephesians 2:13)

All people are separated from God before they are saved. If you have received Jesus Christ as your Savior, you have received the glorious opportunity to continually come closer to God. Be like the apostle Paul who said, "[For my determined purpose is] that I may know Him [that I may progressively become more deeply and intimately acquainted with Him, perceiving and recognizing and understanding the wonders of His Person more strongly and more clearly], and that I may in that same way come to know the power outflowing from His resurrection [which it exerts over believers], and that I may so share His sufferings as to be continually transformed [in spirit into His likeness even] to His death, [in the hope] that if possible I may attain to the [spiritual and moral] resurrection [that lifts me] out from among the dead [even while in the body]." (Philippians 3:10-11)

Paul was determined to know God more intimately. With every passing month and year, Paul wanted to progressively know God more intimately than he did in the past. This verse of Scripture is an excellent definition of the commitment that God is looking for from His children who truly desire to live continually in His presence. "...set your mind and heart to seek (inquire of and require as your vital necessity) the Lord your God...." (I Chronicles 22:19)

The amplification in this verse says that knowing God intimately is a "vital necessity." You cannot live continually in God's presence unless you know Him intimately. Be like the psalmist who said, "My inner self thirsts for God, for the living God..." (Psalm 42:2)

Do these words describe you? Do you thirst for a close and intimate relationship with God? Are you like the psalmist David who spoke the following words when he was in the wilderness? "O God, You are my God, earnestly will I seek You; my inner self thirsts for You, my flesh longs and is faint for You, in a dry and weary land where no water is." (Psalm 63:1)

Do you seek God earnestly? Do you thirst for an intimate relationship with Him? Do you long to know God more intimately? If you can answer these questions affirmatively, you are living the way that Christians live who abide in the presence of God. "...let us be zealous to know the Lord [to appreciate, give heed to, and cherish Him]...." (Hosea 6:3)

When you are zealous about something, you fervently pursue whatever you are zealous about. You are completely devoted to this goal. God said, "...you will seek Me, inquire for, and require Me [as a vital necessity] and find Me when you search for Me with all your heart." (Jeremiah 29:13)

Once again you are told that fervently seeking a more intimate relationship with God is "a vital necessity." Living continually in God's presence is the greatest thing that can happen to any person during his or her life on earth. You can only live continually in God's presence if you search for Him wholeheartedly. "...pursue that consecration and holiness without which no one will [ever] see the Lord." (Hebrews 12:14)

No one will ever see the Lord unless this person pursues consecration and holiness. We discussed consecration in II Corinthians 7:1 earlier in this chapter. Consecration means to devote your life entirely to God. If you truly desire to live continually in God's presence, you will live a holy lifestyle that is continually devoted to knowing God more intimately.

Holiness is the purity of God. Your Father yearns to reveal His holiness to you. You can only experience God's holiness by consistently turning away from everything in the world to live a consecrated and focused life. "Come close to God and He will come close to you...." (James 4:8)

You decide how close you will be to God. God promises to come close to you to the degree that you make the commitment to come close to Him. The holy Scriptures instruct you to be "...alive to God [living in unbroken fellowship with Him] in Christ Jesus." (Romans 6:11)

Please note the words "unbroken fellowship with Him" in the amplification of this verse. Your Father wants you to continually draw closer to Him. You can only live in His presence to the degree that you constantly draw closer to Him.

This chapter is filled with scriptural instructions pertaining to a close and intimate relationship with God and reverent fear and awe toward God. Each chapter in this book will give you more scriptural information about the lifestyle that God desires for you to live if you truly want to partake of the greatest of all privileges during your life on earth – living continually in His presence.

Chapter 4

Receive Supernatural Protection by Living in God's Presence

In this chapter we will study Scripture explaining that God lives in the heart of every person who has received Jesus Christ as his or her Savior. To come into the presence of God, you merely need to turn within yourself. God is omnipresent. He sits on His throne in heaven. He also lives in the heart of every one of His children on earth. "One God and Father of [us] all, Who is above all [Sovereign over all], pervading all and [living] in [us] all." (Ephesians 4:6)

Please note that the word "all" is used five times in this one verse of Scripture and the amplification. God is emphasizing that He lives in the heart of every one of His children. He is on His throne in heaven where He is the Sovereign ruler over the entire universe. God also "pervades" all. The word "pervade" means to be spread out. The same God Who sits on His throne in heaven is spread out all over the world where He lives in the heart of *every one* of His children who have been redeemed by the blood of His Son Jesus Christ.

If Jesus Christ is your Savior, the same God Who created you lives in *your* heart. You can live in His presence continually because He is with you throughout every minute of every hour of every day of your life.

Jesus Christ Who sits on a throne in heaven next to God also lives in your heart if He is your Savior. "May Christ through your faith [actually] dwell (settle down, abide, make His permanent home) in your hearts!...." (Ephesians 3:17)

Your faith in the reliability of God's Word is the key to determining your certainty of Christ's presence in your heart. The amplification says that Jesus makes "His permanent home in your heart."

God is with you continually. Jesus Christ is with you continually. The Holy Spirit also lives in the heart of every person who has received Jesus Christ as his or her Savior. "...God's Spirit has His permanent dwelling in you [to be at home in you, collectively as a church and also individually]..." (I Corinthians 3:16)

We just learned in Ephesians 3:17 that Jesus Christ makes His permanent home in your heart. This verse explains that the Holy Spirit also makes His permanent dwelling in your heart. The Holy Spirit lives collectively in the hearts of all Christians throughout the world and individually in your heart if Jesus Christ is your Savior. "...you are in Him, made full and having come to fullness of life [in Christ you too are filled with the Godhead—Father, Son and Holy Spirit—and reach full spiritual stature]...." (Colossians 2:10)

The amplification at the end of this verse says that you will "reach full spiritual stature" if you are certain that Father, Son and Holy Spirit live in your heart. "...He is not far from each one of us. For in Him we live and move and have our being..." (Acts 17:27-28)

We now are ready to study Scripture pertaining to the relationship between entering into God's rest and living in the presence of God. "...the Lord said, My Presence shall go with you, and I will give you rest." (Exodus 33:14)

Rest in God at all times. *Why* would you ever be concerned about any problem you face if you know that you are in God's presence? There is no safer place in the entire universe than to be in the presence of God. "...the Lord has given you rest from your sorrow and pain and from your trouble and unrest..." (Isaiah 14:3)

God wants you to rest in Him whenever you face "sorrow and pain and trouble." Absolutely refuse to concern yourself with the problems you face. If you know that you are in God's presence, you will be certain that He will take care of everything. "...he who has once entered [God's] rest also has ceased from [the weariness and pain] of human labors..." (Hebrews 4:10)

You will never struggle and strain trying to solve difficult problems with your limited human abilities if you are absolutely certain that you are living in God's presence. You will rest in God. He wants you to rest in Him, placing all of your trust and confidence in Him.

When you are in the presence of God, you will always be quiet, calm and confident deep down inside of yourself. You will be absolutely certain that God is in complete control. God instructs you to "...be calm and cool and steady, accept and suffer unflinchingly every hardship..." (II Timothy 4:5)

Please note the word "every" near the end of this verse. No matter how difficult any problem you face might be, your Father wants you to be "calm and cool and steady." He does not want you to flinch in the face of any adversity. If you are in God's presence, you will be absolutely certain that you are in the safest place in the entire universe. "...whoever leans on, trusts in, and puts his confidence in the Lord is safe and set on high." (Proverbs 29:5)

If you are in God's presence and you trust Him completely, you will be safe at all times. God will elevate you above every problem you face.

We will devote the remainder of this chapter to studying what Psalm 91 teaches about God's protection for every one of His children who continually dwell in His presence. "He who dwells in the secret place of the Most High shall remain stable and fixed under the shadow of the Almighty [Whose power no foe can withstand]." (Psalm 91:1)

God's presence is a secret place because it is unknown to all unbelievers and to many believers. The words "Most High" refer to God. If you dwell (live permanently) in God's presence, you will be "stable and fixed" at all times.

When this verse refers to the shadow of God, it refers to being so close to God in the spiritual realm that you actually are in His shadow. God's supernatural power is much greater than any person or any situation on earth.

There is no question that the words "the secret place" refer to the presence of God. Before we proceed to study Psalm 91 we will look at the words of the psalmist David who said, "In the secret place of Your presence You hide them from the plots of men…" (Psalm 31:20)

This verse confirms that the secret place of the Most High actually is the secret place of God's presence. "I will say of the Lord, He is my Refuge and my Fortress, my God; on Him I lean and rely, and in Him I [confidently] trust!" (Psalm 91:2)

A refuge is a safe place where you are protected. A fortress is a place that has been strengthened to provide significant protection. God wants you to *speak* of your absolute faith and confidence that He is protecting you.

We now will look at one more passage of Scripture from Psalm 91. "A thousand may fall at your side, and ten thousand at your right hand, but it shall not come near you. Only a spectator shall you be [yourself inaccessible in the secret place of the Most High] as you witness the reward of the wicked. Because you have made the Lord your refuge, and the Most High your dwelling place, there shall no evil befall you, nor any plague or calamity come near your tent." (Psalm 91:7-10)

No matter what is taking place in the world around you, you will be protected if you remain in God's presence. You will be "only a spectator" to whatever adversity is occurring. People may be falling all around you, but you will be completely safe when you are in God's presence. "The Lord also will be a refuge and a high tower for the oppressed, a refuge and a stronghold in times of trouble (high cost, destitution, and desperation)." (Psalm 9:9)

We have included this verse because of the words "high cost, destitution, and desperation" in the amplification. We believe that our generation lives in the last days before Jesus Christ returns. Difficult times are coming upon the world (see II Timothy 3:1).

Regardless of how difficult the economic situation might be or how desperate people who trust in worldly sources of security are, you will be sheltered in God if you know Him intimately, trust Him completely and live continually in the safety of His presence. "...in the shadow of Your wings will I take refuge and be confident until calamities and destructive storms are passed." (Psalm 57:1)

Once again, when this verse speaks of being in God's shadow, it refers to being in God's presence. Be filled with unwavering faith in God. Know that God will protect you until every storm has passed.

Chapter 5

Pride Can Keep You Out of the Presence of God

In this chapter we will study Scripture pertaining to the effect that pride and humility have on living in the presence of God. Every person who is born into this world is a descendant of Adam and inherits the tendency to be prideful from Adam. "…all seek [to advance] their own interests, not those of Jesus Christ (the Messiah)." (Philippians 2:21)

Please note the word "all" in this verse. Every person has the tendency to seek his or her own interests. Adam and Eve were proud. They disobeyed God's specific instructions about not eating the forbidden fruit in the Garden of Eden (see Genesis 2:16-17). Their pride, selfishness and disobedience caused them to be separated from God and caused every person born since that time to be born separated from God.

Satan and his demons do everything they can to influence people to be proud. At one time Satan was an archangel in heaven named Lucifer. Lucifer was proud and selfish. He attempted to elevate himself above God.

God cast Lucifer out of heaven because of his pride. "How have you fallen from heaven, O light-bringer and daystar, son of the morning! How you have been cut down to the ground, you who weakened and laid low the nations [O blasphemous, satanic king of Babylon!] And you said in your heart, I will ascend to heaven; I will exalt my throne above the stars of God; I will sit upon the mount of assembly in the uttermost north. I will ascend above the heights of the clouds; I will make myself like the Most High." (Isaiah 14:12-14)

Many angels in heaven were proud. They attempted to follow Lucifer in exalting themselves above God. These angels also were cast out of heaven. "...the huge dragon was cast down and out—that age-old serpent, who is called the Devil and Satan, he who is the seducer (deceiver) of all humanity the world over; he was forced out and down to the earth, and his angels were flung out along with him." (Revelation 12:9)

Adam and Eve were separated from God because of pride. Satan and his demons once were angels. They were separated from God because of pride. Proud people cannot enter into the presence of God.

Humility is essential to entering into the presence of God. "...Clothe (apron) yourselves, all of you, with humility [as the garb of a servant, so that its covering cannot possibly be stripped from you, with freedom from pride and arrogance] toward one another. For God sets Himself against the proud (the insolent, the overbearing, the disdainful, the presumptuous, the boastful)—[and He opposes, frustrates, and defeats them], but gives grace (favor, blessing) to the humble." (I Peter 5:5)

You are instructed to "clothe yourself" with humility so that you will be completely free from pride. When you put clothing on your body, you cover yourself. When you clothe yourself with humility, you are completely covered with humility.

This verse is one of the strongest statements in the Bible about God not wanting us to be proud. The amplification in this verse says that God "opposes, frustrates, and defeats" people who are proud.

God wants each of us to be humble. "...though the Lord is high, yet has He respect to the lowly [bringing them into fellowship with Him]; but the proud and haughty He knows and recognizes [only] at a distance." (Psalm 138:6)

Please note that the amplification of this verse says that God will bring humble people into fellowship with Him. Jesus Christ said, "For everyone who exalts himself will be humbled (ranked below others who are honored or rewarded), and he who humbles himself (keeps a modest opinion of himself and behaves accordingly) will be exalted (elevated in rank)." (Luke 14:11)

Every person who is proud ultimately will be humbled and *brought down*. God *lifts up* His children who truly are humble. Jesus Christ is our example in every area of life. Jesus was very humble throughout His earthly ministry. He said, "...I am gentle (meek) and humble (lowly) in heart..." (Matthew 11:29)

Jesus had no prideful desire to receive recognition from other human beings for the great miracles He performed. He said, "I receive not glory from men [I crave no human honor, I look for no mortal fame]" (John 5:41)

Your Father wants you to be humble just as His beloved Son was humble when He was on earth. "Let this same attitude and purpose and [humble] mind be in you which was in Christ Jesus: [Let Him be your example in humility:]" (Philippians 2:5)

No person has earned the right to come into God's presence. You can partake of the privilege of entering into the presence of God only to the degree that you truly are humble. "…He gives His undeserved favor to the low [in rank], the humble, and the afflicted." (Proverbs 3:34)

This book is filled with specific instructions pertaining to entering into the presence of God. Only Christians who are humble and teachable will pay the price of learning these instructions. "…knowledge is easy to him who [being teachable] understands." (Proverbs 14:6)

Are you willing to cast aside all preconceived opinions to learn new truths from the Word of God? If you have approached this book with a humble and teachable attitude, you will be open to learning exactly what your loving Father instructs you to do to come into His presence. "He leads the humble in what is right, and the humble He teaches His way." (Psalm 25:9)

God will guide you and teach you if you truly are humble. "Who is there among you who is wise and intelligent? Then let him by his noble living show forth his [good] works with the [unobtrusive] humility [which is the proper attribute] of true wisdom." (James 3:13)

If you are truly wise in the Lord, you will be humble and teachable. You will yearn to learn exactly what God says about coming into His presence. You will faithfully obey these instructions.

This chapter contains several Scripture references pertaining to pride and humility. In the next chapter we will look into God's Word for specific instructions pertaining to surrendering control of your life to God and coming into His presence.

Chapter 6

Surrender Control of Your Life

Jesus Christ paid a tremendous price for you when He died a horrible death by crucifixion. He paid this price so that you will give up your God-given right to control your life and willingly surrender control to Him. "...He died for all, so that all those who live might live no longer to and for themselves, but to and for Him Who died and was raised again for their sake." (II Corinthians 5:15)

Jesus Christ died and was raised from the dead for you. Live your life for Jesus, not for yourself. Trust Jesus completely to do in you, through you and for you what you cannot do yourself. "...Believe in the Lord Jesus Christ [give yourself up to Him, take yourself out of your own keeping and entrust yourself into His keeping]..." (Acts 16:31)

Give up control of your life. Trust the Lord Jesus Christ to control your life. "A man's mind plans his way, but the Lord directs his steps and makes them sure." (Proverbs 16:9)

God has given each of us freedom of choice to decide how we will live our lives. He is willing and able to direct your steps to live the way He wants you to live if you will willingly surrender control of your life to Him. Be like the apostle Paul who said, "I have been crucified with Christ [in Him I have shared His crucifixion]; it is no longer I who live, but Christ (the Messiah) lives in me; and the life I now live in the body I live by faith in (by adherence to and reliance on and complete trust in) the Son of God, Who loved me and gave Himself up for me." (Galatians 2:20)

Paul said that he was crucified just as Jesus was crucified. Crucify your God-given ability to control your life. Surrender control of your life completely to Jesus Christ Who lives in your heart if He is your Savior. Jesus will do a much better job of controlling your life than you can do yourself. Jesus said, "Whoever finds his [lower] life will lose it [the higher life], and whoever loses his [lower] life on My account will find it [the higher life]." (Matthew 10:39)

The lower life is the life that you live when you are in control. The higher life is the life that you live when Jesus is in control. The higher life is the life that is lived continually in the presence of God. "...offer and yield yourselves to God as though you have been raised from the dead to [perpetual] life, and your bodily members [and faculties] to God, presenting them as implements of righteousness." (Romans 6:13)

Make an offering of your life to God. Willingly surrender your God-given ability to control your life. Gladly allow God to control your life. Allow your loving Father to shape you and mold you. "...You are our Father; we are the clay, and You our Potter, and we all are the work of Your hand." (Isaiah 64:8)

The Bible teaches that God is the Potter and you are clay. You decide whether you will allow God to shape you and mold you. Your Father is more than willing to shape you and mold you to the degree that you willingly surrender control of your life to Him. "...live and move not in the ways of the flesh but in the ways of the Spirit [our lives governed not by the standards and according to the dictates of the flesh, but controlled by the Holy Spirit]." (Romans 8:4)

Allow the Holy Spirit to govern your life. He can do a much better job of controlling your life than you can. You decide whether you will be in control of your life or whether you will gladly yield control of your life to the Holy Spirit. "...you are living the life of the Spirit, if the [Holy] Spirit of God [really] dwells within you [directs and controls you]...." (Romans 8:9)

The amplification at the end of this verse says that you are living the way God wants you to live if the Holy Spirit "directs and controls" your life. "...walk and live [habitually] in the [Holy] Spirit [responsive to and controlled and guided by the Spirit]..." (Galatians 5:16)

Please note the word "habitually" in the amplification at the beginning of this verse. Allow the Holy Spirit to constantly control your life. "...let us go forward walking in line, our conduct controlled by the Spirit.]" (Galatians 5:25)

God always emphasizes through repetition. We have just studied four verses of Scripture that instruct you to allow the Holy Spirit to control your life.

You are moving backward in your life when you are in control. You will be moving steadily forward if the Holy Spirit controls your life. "Do not quench (suppress or subdue) the [Holy] Spirit" (I Thessalonians 5:19).

Once you begin to live in the Holy Spirit, you will no longer want to live a life that is controlled by the desires of the flesh. The Holy Spirit has the perfect will of God for you if you yield control to Him.

Chapter 7

Only Grateful Christians Live in God's Presence

In this chapter we will study several passages of Scripture that clearly explain why every person on earth should have deep and continued gratitude to God and to Jesus Christ. As you study the Scripture references regarding the enormity of the price that God paid and the price that Jesus Christ paid for you, we believe that your heart will overflow with gratitude. We believe that you often will spontaneously say, "Thank You, Father." "Thank You, Father." "Thank You, Father." and "Thank You, Jesus." "Thank You, Jesus." "Thank You, Jesus."

The remainder of this book will be filled with numerous Scripture references that explain the relationship between consistently thanking God, consistently praising God and entering into God's presence. If you can even begin to comprehend the magnitude of the enormous price that Jesus Christ paid for you, you *will* thank Him and praise Him many times throughout every day and night of your life. If you are deeply grateful to God, you will thank Him and praise Him continually.

We will begin this chapter by studying one of the best-known verses of Scripture in the Bible. "...God so greatly loved and dearly prized the world that He [even] gave up His only begotten (unique) Son, so that whoever believes in (trusts in, clings to, relies on) Him shall not perish (come to destruction, be lost) but have eternal (everlasting) life." (John 3:16)

Please note the words "greatly" and "dearly" in this verse. These words emphasize *how much* God loves every person in the world. God's love is unconditional. He loves the worst sinner just as much as He loves humble, loving and caring Christians. God so greatly loved the world that He willingly gave up His only Son to die an excruciating death by crucifixion.

God paid this enormous price so that every person who receives Jesus Christ as his or her Savior will live throughout eternity with Him in heaven. If you are not certain that you will live throughout eternity in heaven, please stop reading now and turn to the Appendix at the end of this book.

Are you a parent? Can you imagine giving up your only child to a horrible death to pay the price for people who sin? This price is exactly what God paid when He gave His only Son.

If Jesus Christ is your Savior, God is your loving Father. You are His beloved child (see Romans 8:15-16, II Corinthians 6:18, Galatians 3:26, Ephesians 3:14-15 and I John 3:1). As you realize the enormity of the price that God paid, you often will say, "Thank You, Father." "Thank You, Father." "Thank You, Father." "Thank You, Father." "Thank You, Father."

Now that we have studied the one verse of Scripture that above all else explains why your heart should overflow with gratitude to God, we are ready to study additional passages of Scripture that explain why your heart should continually overflow with gratitude. The Bible says that Jesus Christ Who "...although being essentially one with God and in the form of God [possessing the fullness of the attributes which make God God], did not think this equality with God was a thing to be eagerly grasped or retained, but stripped Himself [of all privileges and rightful dignity], so as to assume the guise of a servant (slave), in that He became like men and was born a human being." (Philippians 2:6-7)

Philippians 2:6 tells you that Jesus Christ *is one with God and equal to God.* In spite of this exalted position, Jesus "did not think this equality with God was a thing to be eagerly grasped or retained." Jesus set aside all of the privileges that He had in heaven to come to earth as "a servant, slave" in the form of a human being. "...after He had appeared in human form, He abased and humbled Himself [still further] and carried His obedience to the extreme of death, even the death of the cross!" (Philippians 2:8)

Think of the magnitude of what you have just read. Jesus Christ willingly chose to set aside His position of equality with God in heaven to come to earth as a human being. He then humbled Himself even more by dying a horrible death by crucifixion to pay the full price for all of the sins that every person has ever committed.

Crucifixion was such a severe method of punishment that Roman citizens could not be crucified. Crucifixion was reserved for the very worst criminals from other countries. Jesus Christ, Who left His position of equality with God, paid the *same* price that the worst criminals paid.

Jesus knew the price that He would have to pay. He came to earth as the Son of man (see Matthew 6:20). Although Jesus still was the Son of God, He came to earth as a human being Who had willingly set aside His equality with God in heaven. Jesus chose to live in His earthly ministry as a human being just like you, totally dependent on God.

Jesus experienced great anguish in His humanity as the time for His crucifixion approached. In the Garden of Gethsemane shortly before the time when Jesus would be crucified, "...He fell on the ground and kept praying that if it were possible the [fatal] hour might pass from Him. And He was saying, Abba, [which means] Father, everything is possible for You. Take away this cup from Me; yet not what I will, but what You [will]." (Mark 14:35-36)

Think of the magnitude of the words you have just read. Jesus Christ, Who willingly gave up His position of equality with God in heaven to come to earth as a human being, suffered great anguish in His humanity. He fell to the ground. He prayed to His Father asking Him to take away the horrible price that He soon would pay. However, Jesus said, "not what I will, but what You will."

Jesus was mercilessly whipped by Roman soldiers before He was crucified. Pontius Pilate ordered Jesus to be flogged with a leaded whip. This type of whipping is called scourging where a person is whipped with a lash containing several leather thongs that are weighted with lead pellets and sharp pieces of bone.

Scourging was a such a severe form of punishment that Roman law limited a maximum of 39 strokes with a whip. Even so, many people fainted because of the pain. Some people died.

Jesus was stripped of His clothing before He was flogged by Roman soldiers. His hands were tied to an upright post. Jesus undoubtedly lost a great deal of blood because of the severe whipping. He may have become unconscious.

How badly was the Son of God whipped for *you*? "[For many the Servant of God became an object of horror; many were astonished at Him.] His face and His whole appearance were marred more than any man's, and His form beyond that of the sons of men..." (Isaiah 52:14)

The prophet Isaiah prophesied how badly Jesus would be whipped. Jesus was whipped *so badly* that He "became an object of horror." He took whiplashes across His *face* from these weighted whips for you. People who observed this whipping were astonished at how badly Jesus had been whipped. They were horrified by what they saw. Jesus was whipped so badly that His face and His entire appearance "were marred more than any man's."

A procession of people then went with the bloody and mutilated Jesus Christ to the place where He would be crucified. "...when they came to the place which is called The Skull [Latin: Calvary; Hebrew: Golgotha], there they crucified Him..." (Luke 23:33)

Jesus was thrown to the ground before He was crucified. He was laying on His back with His arms stretched out across the crossbeam of the cross where He would be crucified. Large spikes that were approximately seven inches long were driven into His wrists. Jesus then was lifted to the permanent upright portion of the cross where Roman soldiers then nailed His ankles to the cross with more large spikes.

Jesus suffered through three agonizing hours nailed to that cross to pay the full price for *your* sins. Jesus agonized on that cross from approximately noon on what we today call Good Friday until approximately 3:00 p.m.

As His agonizing time on the cross drew to a close, Jesus suddenly realized that His Father had *abandoned* Him. "...about the ninth hour (three o'clock) Jesus cried with a loud voice, Eli, Eli, lama sabachthani?—that is, My God, My God, why have You abandoned Me [leaving Me helpless, forsaking and failing Me in My need]?" (Matthew 27:46)

Why did God abandon His Son? "For our sake He made Christ [virtually] to be sin Who knew no sin, so that in and through Him we might become [endued with, viewed as being in, and examples of] the righteousness of God [what we ought to be, approved and acceptable and in right relationship with Him, by His goodness]." (II Corinthians 5:21)

Jesus Christ lived a perfect life throughout His earthly ministry. He never sinned. Nevertheless, He *became sin* to pay the full price for the sins of every person in the world. Jesus became black with sin when He took upon Himself the sins of every person. God could not look upon the blackness of the sin of the entire world. He was forced to turn away from His Son.

Is your heart filled with gratitude as you see the enormity of the price that Jesus Christ paid for *your* sins? Is your mouth opening to say "Thank You, Jesus" ... "Thank You, Jesus." "Thank You, Jesus," "Thank You, Jesus." "Thank You, Jesus." again and again?

In the remainder of this book we will carefully study what the Word of God teaches about the relationship between deep gratitude to God, continually thanking God, continually praising God and living in the presence of God.

Chapter 8

Thank God Continually

If you have deep gratitude to God, you will thank Him continually. The Bible explains that we come into God's presence when we thank Him. "Let us come before His presence with thanksgiving; let us make a joyful noise to Him with songs of praise!" (Psalm 95:2)

You will see in the next four chapters that the Bible repeatedly teaches that we will come into God's presence when we thank Him and praise Him. "Enter into His gates with thanksgiving and a thank offering and into His courts with praise! Be thankful and say so to Him, bless and affectionately praise His name!" (Psalm 100:4)

This verse explains that you will enter into the gates of God's courtyard if you continually thank Him. The Hebrew word "shaar" that is translated as "gates" in this verse means an opening. Thanking God continually opens the way for you to come into God's presence. The words "thank offering" means that you are making an offering to God when you thank Him continually. If you are deeply grateful to God, you will consistently thank Him and praise Him. You will consistently be in His presence.

You will go from the gates into God's courts if you praise Him continually. If you truly are thankful, you will say so to God. You will "bless and affectionately praise His name."

In this chapter we will study several verses of Scripture about thanking God. In subsequent chapters we will study many additional verses of Scripture about praising God. "Now thanks be to God for His Gift, [precious] beyond telling [His indescribable, inexpressible, free Gift]!" (II Corinthians 9:15)

The amplification in this verse explains that God's free Gift of Jesus Christ is *so* great that we cannot describe it. Our human vocabulary does not contain words that can even begin to explain the enormity of the Gift that God gave to the world when He sent His beloved Son to earth to pay the full price for the sins of every person.

God gave you a tremendous gift when He willingly gave up His only Son. Jesus Christ gave you a tremendous gift when He took *your* place on the cross and paid the full price for *your* sins. Thank God continually for this precious Gift. Thank Jesus for the enormous price that He paid.

We also are instructed to thank God for His goodness, His mercy and His loving-kindness. "O give thanks to the Lord, for He is good; for His mercy and loving-kindness endure forever. O give thanks to the God of gods, for His mercy and loving-kindness endure forever. O give thanks to the Lord of lords, for His mercy and loving-kindness endure forever" (Psalm 136:1-3)

God always emphasizes through repetition. When God repeats the same words in three consecutive verses, you can be certain that He is placing significant emphasis on these words. God's mercy and loving-kindness endure forever. Thank God continually for His mercy, His love and His kindness to you. God further emphasizes this principle by giving us the exact same instruction in Psalm 107:11 and Jeremiah 33:11.

Follow the advice of the apostle Paul in his first letter to the Thessalonians when he said, "...we also [especially] thank God continually for this, that when you received the message of God [which you heard] from us, you welcomed it not as the word of [mere] men, but as it truly is, the Word of God, which is effectually at work in you who believe [exercising its superhuman power in those who adhere to and trust in and rely on it]." (I Thessalonians 2:13)

Paul emphasized the importance of thanking God continually for His Word. The Bible is not "the word of mere men." God is the Author of the Bible. Every word written by the human authors of the Bible was anointed by God (see II Timothy 3:16). The amplification in this verse explains that the Bible contains "superhuman power." The supernatural power of God is released to God's children who "adhere to and trust in and rely on" His Word.

If you can understand the magnitude of the supernatural power of God's Word, you will thank Him continually for His Word. "...He has bestowed on us His precious and exceedingly great promises, so that through them you may escape [by flight] from the moral decay (rottenness and corruption) that is in the world because of covetousness (lust and greed), and become sharers (partakers) of the divine nature." (II Peter 1:4)

The promises in God's Word are described as being "precious and exceedingly great." These promises are so great that they far exceed anything that we can begin to comprehend with our limited human understanding. The promises in God's Word enable you to escape from the moral decay that pervades the world today.

If you continually study and meditate on the Word of God and seek to know Him, you will partake of the nature of God Himself. You will become more and more like God if you obey His instructions to study His Word continually and to meditate on His Word continually (see II Corinthians 4:16, Ephesians 4:22-23, Joshua 1:8 and Psalm 1:2-3).

We have *so much* to thank God for. If you understand the many ways that God has blessed you, you will thank Him continually and you will come into His presence continually. "Thank [God] in everything [no matter what the circumstances may be, be thankful and give thanks], for this is the will of God for you [who are] in Christ Jesus [the Revealer and Mediator of that will]." (I Thessalonians 5:18)

You are instructed to thank God in everything, no matter what circumstances you face. Know that God will cause everything to work out for the best if you continue to thank Him and trust Him completely (see Romans 8:28). The psalmist said, "I will offer to You the sacrifice of thanksgiving and will call on the name of the Lord." (Psalm 116:17)

When you offer to God a sacrifice of thanksgiving, you thank Him in the midst of adversity when you, in your humanity, do not feel like giving thanks to Him. Make the sacrifice of thanking God continually regardless of what is happening in your life. "...thanks be to God, Who in Christ always leads us in triumph [as trophies of Christ's victory]..." (II Corinthians 2:14)

Please note the words "always leads us in triumph" in this verse. Jesus Christ won a victory that is so great that you *always* will walk in His victory if you know God's promises pertaining to His victory and if you persevere with absolute faith in these promises for as long as God requires you to persevere.

Thank God whenever you face adversity because you are certain that Jesus Christ always will lead you in triumph because of the victory that He won when He rose from death after dying on the cross. Jesus said, "...In the world you have tribulation and trials and distress and frustration; but be of good cheer [take courage; be confident, certain, undaunted]! For I have overcome the world. [I have deprived it of power to harm you and have conquered it for you.]" (John 16:33)

Jesus told you to expect to face trials and tribulation in life. He then went on to tell you to "be of good cheer" in the face of adversity. Absolutely *refuse* to allow adversity to overcome you because you are certain that Jesus has deprived anything in the world from being able to harm you.

Meditate continually on these magnificent supernatural words whenever you face adversity. Thank Jesus again and again for the supernatural victory that He has given to you. "...whatever is born of God is victorious over the world; and this is the victory that conquers the world, even our faith. Who is it that is victorious over [that conquers] the world but he who believes that Jesus is the Son of God [who adheres to, trusts in, and relies on that fact]?" (I John 5:4-5)

Every Christian who has been born again shares in the victory that Jesus Christ won over the world. Absolutely refuse to give up. Persevere in your faith in God's supernatural promises pertaining to His Son's victory. You can be certain that God sent His only Son to earth to die on the cross and to rise from the dead to give *you* a supernatural victory over every problem you will ever face.

Absolutely refuse to allow any problem you face to stop you from thanking God. The apostle Paul said, "...amid all these things we are more than conquerors and gain a surpassing victory through Him Who loved us. For I am persuaded beyond doubt (am sure) that neither death nor life, nor angels nor principalities, nor things impending and threatening nor things to come, nor powers, nor height nor depth, nor anything else in all creation will be able to separate us from the love of God which is in Christ Jesus our Lord." (Romans 8:37-39)

Please note the words "all," "more than" and surpassing" at the beginning of this passage of Scripture. You have been given a tremendous victory over every problem you will ever face. This victory surpasses any other victory that has ever been won. Nothing can separate you from the love of God.

Come into God's presence and stay in His presence by thanking Him at all times, regardless of the severity of whatever problems you face. "Do not fret or have any anxiety about anything, but in every circumstance and in everything, by prayer and petition (definite requests), with thanksgiving, continue to make your wants known to God." (Philippians 4:6)

God instructs you not to be anxious about *anything*. No matter how severe any adversity may be, your Father instructs you to come to Him in prayer.

God instructs you to thank Him when you pray because you are certain that He will bring you safely through whatever adversity you face. If you have deep, strong and unwavering faith in God, you will not wait to thank Him until after He has answered your prayer. You will thank God *when you pray*.

The next verse explains what God promises to do if you obey these specific instructions. "...God's peace [shall be yours, that tranquil state of a soul assured of its salvation through Christ, and so fearing nothing from God and being content with its earthly lot of whatever sort that is, that peace] which transcends all understanding shall garrison and mount guard over your hearts and minds in Christ Jesus." (Philippians 4:7)

If you obey God's instructions to thank Him continually, you will experience His supernatural peace. God's peace is so great that it transcends all human understanding. God's peace will guard your mind and your heart if you obey His instructions to thank Him at all times, regardless of the severity of the problems you face.

In this chapter we have studied several passages of Scripture that instruct you to thank God continually. You have seen that you will come into God's presence if you thank Him continually, regardless of the severity of the problems you face.

God's ways are very different and very much higher than the ways of human beings (see Isaiah 55:8-9). Thank God and keep on thanking Him at all times. You can be certain that you will come into God's presence if you do.

Chapter 9

Praise God Continually

In the last chapter we studied several passages of Scripture that explain the relationship between thanking God continually and coming into God's presence. In this chapter we will study Scripture references that explain what the Bible teaches about praising God continually and living in God's presence. "...You are holy, O You Who dwell in [the holy place where] the praises of Israel [are offered]." (Psalm 22:3)

When the Israelites praised God, their praise brought them into the holy place where God was. This same spiritual principle applies to your life today. Continual praise will keep you in God's presence.

Please note the words "dwell in" in this verse of Scripture. When you dwell in a place, this place is your permanent residence. There is no better place to be during our lives on earth than to be in the presence of God. When you praise God, you are doing exactly what God created you to do. He said, "The people I formed for Myself, that they may set forth My praise [and they shall do it]." (Isaiah 43:21)

What could be more important than to do what God created you to do? God created you to praise Him. The psalmist David said, "Great is the Lord and highly to be praised; and His greatness is [so vast and deep as to be] unsearchable." (Psalm 145:3)

God is *so* great that we cannot even begin to comprehend the magnitude of His greatness with the limitations of our human understanding. God is highly deserving of our praise. Praise God for the great things that He does. Praise God for Who He is. "Praise Him for His mighty acts; praise Him according to the abundance of His greatness!" (Psalm 150:2)

God is great, mighty, magnificent and awesome. If you are in absolute awe of God, you will praise Him continually. The psalmist David said, "You who fear (revere and worship) the Lord, praise Him!..." (Psalm 22:23)

When you fear God, you revere Him with awe. He is at the center of your life. Every aspect of your life revolves around Him. Be like the psalmist who said, "Let the peoples praise You [turn away from their idols] and give thanks to You, O God; let all the peoples praise and give thanks to You." (Psalm 67:3)

Please note the words "turn away from their idols" in the amplification of this verse. Christians who focus primarily on things in the world do not praise God and thank Him continually.

God always emphasizes through repetition. Two verses later God emphasizes the same principle that was emphasized in Psalm 67:3. "Let the peoples praise You [turn away from their idols] and give thanks to You,

O God; let all the peoples praise and give thanks to You!" (Psalm 67:5)

You are instructed to turn away from anything in the world that you might allow to come ahead of God in your life. The Bible consistently instructs every person on earth to praise God. "Let everything that has breath and every breath of life praise the Lord! Praise the Lord! (Hallelujah!)" (Psalm 150:6)

If you are alive, you are breathing. Every person on earth who is breathing is instructed to praise God. The Bible repeatedly instructs you to live a life where praising God is a way of life to you.

If your heart is filled with gratitude to God, praising Him will be an ingrained part of your life. If your life is centered around God instead of being centered around people, places or events in the world and your heart is filled with gratitude, you will praise God continually. "From the rising of the sun to the going down of it and from east to west, the name of the Lord is to be praised!" (Psalm 113:3)

Do not limit your praise. Praise God continually throughout every day and night of your life. The words "from east to west" instruct you to praise God no matter where you are. Be like the psalmist who said, "My mouth shall be filled with Your praise and with Your honor all the day." (Psalm 71:8)

The Bible teaches that the words that consistently flow out of our mouths are determined by whatever we truly believe in our hearts. Jesus Christ said, "...out of the fullness (the overflow, the superabundance) of the heart the mouth speaks." (Matthew 12:34)

If your heart is *filled* with gratitude toward God, this gratitude will be expressed by a continual outpouring of praise to God. You will be like the psalmist David who said, "I will bless the Lord at all times; His praise shall continually be in my mouth." (Psalm 34:1)

You bless God when you praise Him. You give God the glory and honor that He so richly deserves. "...let us constantly and at all times offer up to God a sacrifice of praise, which is the fruit of lips that thankfully acknowledge and confess and glorify His name." (Hebrews 13:15)

Thanking God and praising Him is easy when everything is going well in your life. This verse instructs you to continually offer up to God "a sacrifice of praise." We studied this principle when we studied Psalm 116:17 in the last chapter where you are instructed to offer to God a sacrifice of thanksgiving. When you make a sacrifice of praise, you obey God's instructions to praise Him even when you are confronted with adversity that is so severe that you do not feel like praising Him.

When you feel the least like praising God often is the time when you should praise Him the most. If you have absolute faith that God will do everything that His Word promises He will do, you will praise Him continually regardless of whether or not you feel like praising Him. If you praise God consistently in the face of severe adversity, this sacrifice of praise gives clear evidence of your deep gratitude toward God and your strong and unwavering faith in God.

God made the supreme sacrifice when He sent His beloved Son to earth to die an agonizing death by crucifixion and to take upon Himself the sins of the entire world. Jesus Christ made the supreme sacrifice when He left His position of equality with God in heaven to come to earth as a human being to die an agonizing death by crucifixion. Make the commitment that your life will be a continual sacrifice to God by thanking Him and praising Him continually regardless of the circumstances you face.

Jesus Christ won an overwhelming victory that is far beyond the limitations of human comprehension. If you truly understand what the Bible teaches about the magnitude of the victory that Jesus Christ won for you, you will praise Him and thank Him in the face of adversity. In the last chapter we studied the emphasis that Jesus placed when He said that He has overcome every problem you will face in the world (see John 16:33).

How can people get more excited when an athletic team wins a contest than they are about the greatest victory that has ever been won? What do many people do when their team scores a winning goal? These people clap their hands and raise their hands in the air because they are so filled with joy because their team won the game. The Bible teaches you to lift up your hands in praise to God. "Lift up your hands in holiness and to the sanctuary and bless the Lord [affectionately and gratefully praise Him]!" (Psalm 134:2)

You bless God when you praise Him and lift up your hands in holy praise to Him. You are praising God continually because of the greatest victory that has ever been won – the victory that Jesus Christ won when He rose from death.

Express your faith in God by praising Him continually. Be like the psalmist who said, "...You are my hope; O Lord God, You are my trust from my youth and the source of my confidence. Upon You have I leaned and relied from birth; You are He Who took me from my mother's womb and You have been my benefactor from that day. My praise is continually of You." (Psalm 71:5-6)

The psalmist was brought up to trust God from the time he was a young child. You can trust your Father completely to watch over you and to take care of you (see Deuteronomy 31:8, Proverbs 29:25, Isaiah 41:13 and Hebrews 13:5).

If you have obeyed God's instructions to renew your mind in His Word every day and to meditate day and night on the holy Scriptures (see II Corinthians 4:16, Ephesians 4:22-23, Joshua 1:8 and Psalm 1:1-3), you will praise God because you are in such awe of His supernatural Word. You will be like the psalmist who said, "In God, Whose word I praise, in the Lord, Whose word I praise, in God have I put my trust and confident reliance; I will not be afraid." (Psalm 56:10-11)

You will praise the Word of God if you are in absolute awe of the holy Scriptures. God said, "...this is the man to whom I will look and have regard: he who is humble and of a broken or wounded spirit, and who trembles at My word and reveres My commands." (Isaiah 66:2)

Your Father wants you to have so much awe for His supernatural Word that you actually tremble because of your reverence for His Word. Praise God continually because of the supernatural promises in His Word.

If you praise God continually in the face of adversity, your faith in God will be strengthened. You will be like Abraham. "No unbelief or distrust made him waver (doubtingly question) concerning the promise of God, but he grew strong and was empowered by faith as he gave praise and glory to God" (Romans 4:20)

Abraham did not allow his faith in God to waver because of doubt and unbelief concerning God's promises. Your faith in God will be strengthened if you consistently give praise to God at all times, regardless of the circumstances you face. Jesus Christ was sent to earth to give you "...beauty instead of ashes, the oil of joy instead of mourning, the garment [expressive] of praise instead of a heavy, burdened, and failing spirit" (Isaiah 61:3)

Do not have a "heavy, burdened and failing spirit" because you are tempted to be discouraged by the problems you face. The Bible compares praise to a garment that covers your body. You are instructed to cover yourself with praise at all times just as your body is covered by your clothing.

If you obey these instructions, God will give you His beauty and His joy instead of the "ashes" that you will experience if you allow adversity to overwhelm you. "As the refining pot for silver and the furnace for gold [bring forth all the impurities of the metal], so let a man be in his trial of praise [ridding himself of all that is base or insincere; for a man is judged by what he praises and of what he boasts]." (Proverbs 27:21)

Impurities in silver and gold are removed by heat. This same principle applies when you face severe adversity. If you react to adversity by sacrificially praising God, this reaction will clearly indicate that you trust God completely.

This verse compares the refining of gold and silver through heat with what will take place in your life if you praise God continually when you face adversity. When this verse of Scripture was written, silver was purified in a refining pot and gold was put into a furnace to remove impurities. As the impurities in gold and silver are removed by severe heat, you will be cleansed "of all that is base or insincere" if you praise God continually in the face of adversity.

Continually praising God in the face of adversity clearly indicates your complete trust in God. Continually praising God regardless of whatever circumstances you face cleanses you spiritually.

You saw in the last chapter that thanking God brings you into God's presence. We studied Psalm 22:3 at the beginning of this chapter where you are told that God is present in the praises of His people. Thank God and praise God continually because of your deep gratitude toward Him.

Chapter 10

Sing Praise to God Continually

In the next two chapters we will study several passages of Scripture pertaining to *singing* praise to God. Most churches have a time of praise and worship at the beginning of their services.

Many Christians who attend a worship service do not truly worship God from their hearts. They sing, repeating the words of the songs that are posted, but they are not totally focused on the words they are singing. Their praise does not flow out of a heart that is filled with gratitude.

When you are praising and worshiping God in church, think about the words you are singing. Personalize your praise and worship to God. Do not just mouth words from familiar songs or the words of the worship music that are posted for the congregation to read.

You can experience the presence of God in a church worship service if your songs of praise to God flow out of a heart that is filled with gratitude. If your heart is filled with gratitude to God, you will express the joy in your heart by singing praises to God. "Make a joyful noise to the Lord, all you lands! Serve the Lord with gladness! Come before His presence with singing!" (Psalm 100:1-2)

Every person is instructed to "make a joyful noise to the Lord." If you are singing words of praise in church or any other place from a heart that is filled with gratitude, you can and will come into God's presence "with singing." "Blessed (happy, fortunate, to be envied) are those who dwell in Your house and Your presence; they will be singing Your praises all the day long." (Psalm 84:4)

This verse instructs you to *dwell* in God's house and God's presence. When you dwell in a place, this place is your permanent residence. We saw in Chapter 1 that you can live *continually* in the presence of God (see I Chronicles 16:11). If you want to achieve this awesome goal, sing praise to God "all the day long."

Do not reserve singing praise to God for when you are in church. Sing praise to God often. The more often you sing praise to God, the more you will come into His presence. "Make a joyful noise unto God, all the earth; sing forth the honor and glory of His name; make His praise glorious!" (Psalm 66:1-2)

Please note the words "all the earth" in this passage of Scripture. God's Word instructs everyone to make a joyful noise when they praise God. Be like the psalmist David who said, "So will I sing praise to Your name forever, paying my vows day by day." (Psalm 61:8)

Sing praise to God often because of your tremendous gratitude to Him for Who He is and for everything He does in your life. The psalmist said, "...You, O

Lord, have made me glad by Your works; at the deeds of Your hands I joyfully sing." (Psalm 92:4)

God is more than worthy of your praise. Sing praises to Him with joy. "Praise the Lord! For the Lord is good; sing praises to His name, for He is gracious and lovely!" (Psalm 135:3)

Several psalms instruct us to *sing* praises to God. The psalmist David said, "...I have trusted, leaned on, and been confident in Your mercy and loving-kindness; my heart shall rejoice and be in high spirits in Your salvation. I will sing to the Lord, because He has dealt bountifully with me." (Psalm 13:5-6)

If you continually sing praise to God, you will remain in His presence. If you truly trust God and have deep, strong and unwavering confidence in Him, your heart will sing with joy regardless of the circumstances you face.

David repeatedly emphasized singing praise to God. He said, "The Lord is my Strength and my [impenetrable] Shield; my heart trusts in, relies on, and confidently leans on Him, and I am helped; therefore my heart greatly rejoices, and with my song will I praise Him." (Psalm 28:7)

God will help you if you persevere in faith, no matter how long any problem lasts until it is resolved (see Hebrews 6:12). Rejoice and sing praises to God regardless of the circumstances you face. If you deeply believe in the reliability of the promises in God's Word and place all of your trust and reliance on God and the authenticity of His promises, you will sing praise to Him (see Numbers 23:19, Joshua 23:14, Jeremiah 1:12, I Corinthians 1:9 and II Corinthians 1:20).

Sing praise to God whenever you face a challenge that seems to have no solution. The psalmist said, "My heart is fixed, O God, my heart is steadfast and confident! I will sing and make melody." (Psalm 57:7)

Your heart will be "fixed" if your heart is filled with the Word of God as a result of consistent Scripture meditation. You will remain in God's presence. Your faith in God will be steady and unwavering, regardless of the severity of the circumstances you face.

If your heart is fixed because your heart is filled with unwavering faith in God, you will sing praises to God. In the next chapter we will study two very important passages of Scripture that explain the enormous power of singing songs of praise to God with absolute faith in Him when you face adversity.

Chapter 11

Sing Praise to God When You Face Adversity

Singing praises to God in the face of adversity is a strong indication of your faith in God. Doing this releases supernatural power in the spiritual realm. The apostle Paul and his friend Silas were put into a prison in Philippi because they had told many people that Jesus Christ is the Messiah. "The crowd [also] joined in the attack upon them, and the rulers tore the clothes off of them and commanded that they be beaten with rods. And when they had struck them with many blows, they threw them into prison, charging the jailer to keep them safely. He, having received [so strict a] charge, put them into the inner prison (the dungeon) and fastened their feet in the stocks." (Acts 16:22-24)

Paul and Silas were attacked. Their clothes were torn from them. They were beaten. They were thrown into prison. Their hands and feet were held by chains.

How did Paul and Silas react to these despicable conditions? Did they feel sorry for themselves? They did not. "...about midnight, as Paul and Silas were praying and singing hymns of praise to God, and the [other] prisoners were listening to them, suddenly there was a great earthquake, so that the very foundations of the prison were shaken; and at once all the doors were opened and everyone's shackles were unfastened." (Acts 16:25-26)

A mighty earthquake occurred when Paul and Silas were praying and singing praise to God. This earthquake was so powerful that the foundations of the prison were shaken. All of the doors of the prison were opened. Every prisoner was set free.

Do not underestimate the supernatural power of continually singing praise to God when you face adversity. Remain in God's presence. Show your faith in God by singing praise to Him regardless of the severity of any problem you face. Sing songs of praise even though doing this may be the last thing you feel like doing.

Meditate on Acts 16:25-26 about Paul and Silas continually singing praise to God. Know that God will honor your faith if you sing praises to Him instead of complaining.

The Bible gives us another example of the supernatural power of singing praise to God in the face of adversity. Chapter 20 of II Chronicles explains the severe adversity that King Jehoshaphat and his followers faced. The king said, "...we have no might to stand against this great company that is coming against us. We do not know what to do, but our eyes are upon You." (II Chronicles 20:12)

King Jehoshaphat refused to focus on the mighty army that was coming against him and his people. He focused continually on God. God responded by speaking through a prophet who said, "...Hearken, all Judah, you inhabitants of Jerusalem, and you King Jehoshaphat. The Lord says this to you: Be not afraid or dismayed at this great multitude; for the battle is not yours, but God's." (II Chronicles 20:15)

Remain in God's presence. Keep your attention focused on Him. Do not give in to fear. Trust God to fight battles that you cannot fight with your limited human abilities.

King Jehoshaphat and his followers praised God in the face of adversity. "...Jehoshaphat bowed his head with his face to the ground, and all Judah and the inhabitants of Jerusalem fell down before the Lord, worshiping Him. And some Levites of the Kohathites and Korahites stood up to praise the Lord, the God of Israel, with a very loud voice." (II Chronicles 20:18-19)

The next morning the king and his followers went out to meet their enemy in a way that showed their faith in God. "...they rose early in the morning and went out into the Wilderness of Tekoa; and as they went out, Jehoshaphat stood and said, Hear me, O Judah, and you inhabitants of Jerusalem! Believe in the Lord your God and you shall be established; believe and remain steadfast to His prophets and you shall prosper. When he had consulted with the people, he appointed singers to sing to the Lord and praise Him in their holy [priestly] garments as they went out before the army, saying, Give thanks to the Lord, for His mercy and loving-kindness endure forever!" (II Chronicles 20:20-21)

King Jehoshaphat and his followers faced an overwhelmingly superior opponent by singing songs of praise and thanking God. How did God respond?

"...when they began to sing and to praise, the Lord set ambushments against the men of Ammon, Moab, and Mount Seir who had come against Judah, and they were [self-] slaughtered" (II Chronicles 20:22)

Follow the example of Paul and Silas and King Jehoshaphat. Instead of giving in to adversity, sing praise to God. The psalmist David said, "...I am poor, sorrowful, and in pain; let Your salvation, O God, set me up on high. I will praise the name of God with a song and will magnify Him with thanksgiving" (Psalm 69:29-30).

The first seven words in this passage of Scripture describe David's reaction to the severity of the problems he faced. How did David respond to this severe adversity? He praised the name of God with a song and magnified God with thanksgiving.

God always emphasizes through repetition. Your Father repeatedly instructs you to sing praise to Him when you face severe adversity. "Is anyone among you afflicted (ill-treated, suffering evil)? He should pray. Is anyone glad at heart? He should sing praise [to God]." (James 5:13)

Pray to God in faith when you face adversity. Is your heart filled with gratitude to God and to Jesus Christ? Show your gratitude by singing praise to God. "Make a joyful noise to the Lord, all the earth; break forth and sing for joy, yes, sing praises!" (Psalm 98:4)

Please note the words "all the earth" in this verse. Every person on earth is instructed to sing praises to God. You will remain in the supernatural presence of God if you consistently obey these instructions.

We often say that God emphasizes through repetition. When your Father gives you the same instruction four times in one verse of Scripture, you can be *certain* that He is emphasizing this instruction to you. "Sing praises to God, sing praises! Sing praises to our King, sing praises! For God is the King of all the earth; sing praises in a skillful psalm and with understanding." (Psalm 47:6-7)

There is no doubt that God wants you to sing praises to Him. He would not have placed this much emphasis on singing praise to Him if singing praise was not extremely important.

Sing praises to God. Your Father will honor you for obeying His specific instructions in this area. "...ever be filled and stimulated with the [Holy] Spirit. Speak out to one another in psalms and hymns and spiritual songs, offering praise with voices [and instruments] and making melody with all your heart to the Lord, at all times and for everything giving thanks in the name of our Lord Jesus Christ to God the Father." (Ephesians 5:18-20)

You will be filled with the Holy Spirit if you consistently sing praise to God and thank Him. The Holy Spirit will be in control of your life, not you.

Please note that the final amplification in this verse instructs you to sing your praise with the accompaniment of musical instruments. In the next two chapters we will give you many specific suggestions about singing praise to God with musical accompaniment. "It is a good and delightful thing to give thanks to the Lord, to sing praises [with musical accompaniment] to Your name, O Most High" (Psalm 92:1)

Once again, please note the amplification instructing you to sing praise to God "with musical accompaniment." "Sing praises to the Lord with the lyre, with the lyre and the voice of melody. With trumpets and the sound of the horn make a joyful noise before the King, the Lord!" (Psalm 98:5-6)

This verse refers to singing praise with a lyre. A lyre is a small stringed instrument that is similar to a harp. This instrument was used to accompany singers. Trumpets and horns also were used to accompany songs of praise when this passage of Scripture was written.

I have found from personal experience over the years that the effectiveness of singing praise to God is increased *greatly* when I consistently sing praise with musical accompaniment. "Praise Him with trumpet sound; praise Him with lute and harp! Praise Him with tambourine and [single or group] dance; praise Him with stringed and wind instruments or flutes! Praise Him with resounding cymbals; praise Him with loud clashing cymbals!" (Psalm 150:3-5)

This passage of Scripture instructed the people to use the instruments that were predominant in their culture at that time. In the next two chapters we will give you specific advice based on practical experience in regard to singing praise to God with musical accompaniment.

Chapter 12

An Effective Way to Sing Praise to God

In the last two chapters we have studied several Scripture references that explain the relationship between singing praise to God and entering into God's presence. In this chapter I will explain how the Holy Spirit led me into a way of life where I constantly have sung praise to God for more than 20 years.

We all are different. When I explain what I have done in regard to singing praise to God for such a long time, some readers will not want to make this type of commitment. Some readers will apply some of the things I have done, but not all of the concepts that I will explain in this chapter.

For the first 18 years after I was saved, I confined singing praise to God to the times when I attended church. Approximately 22 years ago I was watching a program on a Christian television network. The subsequent program featured a man named Bill Gaither and other people singing praise to God. I decided to watch this program. This decision was the beginning of a significant change in my life.

I was so interested in the anointed worship music on this program that I immediately called the 800 number to order my first Gaither video. When I received the first video, I liked it so much that I ordered more. I kept ordering. Today I have almost 300 Christian worship videos from the Gaithers and many other sources.

Whenever I watch a worship video for the first time, I rank this video A+, A or A-. I give any video that ranks below A- to a thrift store. I file the videos in two bookcases in our home according to rank. I can turn at any time to an A+ Christian worship video.

I have learned from experience that I can enjoy an A+ video approximately twice each year. I have a sticker on each video where I post the last date I watched this video. I never tire of watching these A+ videos. When I watch a video after six months, doing this is almost like watching a new video.

I used to spend my evenings watching television like most people. Today, after having so much experience with watching and singing along with Christian worship music, I do not watch television anywhere near as much as I did in the past. I watch selected sporting events, the weather and some Christian television programming.

When I watch sporting events and the weather, I still am not pleased with what comes onto the screen and into my eyes. I mute the commercials. I do not want all of the worldliness that comes from these commercials to enter into my ears. Jesus Christ said, "...Be careful what you are hearing..." (Mark 4:24)

Instead of watching television, I watch worship videos almost 250 nights each year. I sing praise to the

Lord along with many of the worship songs on the videos that I watch.

I have watched some of my Christian worship videos more than 15 times. I always enjoy watching these videos. I do not just repeat the words of the song. I often substitute my own heartfelt words of praise and worship to accompany the music in whatever song I am watching.

In the last chapter we studied several Scripture references where the amplification instructs us to sing praise to God with musical accompaniment. As the years have gone by, I find myself entering more and more into the presence of God as I repeatedly sing along with the videos.

There were no DVDs when I first started watching praise and worship videos. All of my early worship videos were VHS tapes. I now purchase DVDs which I enjoy more than VHS because they are much more flexible. I can carefully select whatever song I want to sing along with and fast-forward past the remainder. Doing this enables me to make all DVDs into A+ DVDs.

Watching and singing praise and worship to God with Christian worship videos has become a way of life to me. I can hardly remember what my evenings used to be like when I watched secular television programs. I look forward to watching carefully selected praise and worship videos. On any given night I have at least 20 A+ videos from which to choose.

In addition to my large selection of worship videos, I have almost *60 hours* of worship music on cassette tapes. When I started my collection of worship music for my car, there were no CDs. By the time I go through almost 60 hours of worship music in my car, I am ready to start over again. I have repeated this cycle for more than 20 years.

When I turn on the ignition in my car, praise and worship music begins immediately. I often am singing praise to God along with the tape before I am out of my driveway. I sing along with praise and worship music most of the time I am in my car. I don't even know how my car radio works. Wherever I am and whatever I am doing in my car, my ears are constantly flooded with magnificent praise and worship music.

I am 83 years old now. I don't drive anywhere near as much as I did in the past. I can remember several business trips when I lived in New Hampshire that required two or more hours of driving time. I really enjoyed singing along with the praise and worship music on these trips.

Almost every day I drive to a beautiful spot near our home that looks out onto the Gulf of Mexico. I spend an hour or more there enjoying the beauty of God's creation, praying to God and praising Him.

I drive approximately 15 minutes each day to and from this beautiful place. This means that I spend approximately 30 minutes each day listening to and singing along with worship music in my car.

I obviously cannot raise my hands in praise to God when I am driving as I often do at home, but I sometimes raise one hand as I sing along with the worship music. One time I raised my hand in praise and a man on the street waved at me.

When I was younger, I often was impatient waiting for a traffic light. Just the opposite is true now. When I wait for the light to change, I have additional time to worship God and sing praise to Him.

Over the years I also have played worship music while I was doing routine tasks at my desk such as organizing for the upcoming day and paying bills. When I am doing anything that does not require undivided attention, I often sing along with praise and worship music.

I do my very best to take full advantage of the opportunity to fill what otherwise would be empty time by singing praise to God. The time that I spend in my car or doing miscellaneous tasks at my desk has become a beautiful time of singing praise to God.

Today's technology enables you to listen to worship music through CDs, MP3s, internet radio, smart phones and other devices. I recommend that you find whatever method works best for you. Use this time each day to sing praise to God along with anointed musical accompaniment.

Judy likes classical praise. She has instrumental praise playing while she is working at her desk. She also sings the songs as she is praying them to God.

You may or may not be interested in going to the extremes that I have gone to in watching Christian worship videos and singing along with Christian music in your car. If you have any interest in doing these things, I have devoted the next chapter entirely to specific praise and worship DVDs that I recommend based on more than 20 years of singing praise to God more than 250 evenings each year.

Chapter 13

Recommended Praise and Worship DVDs

In this chapter I have listed DVDs that I recommend. If you have any interest in doing what I do, you might want to order two or three DVDs from this list. See for yourself if you like them. If you do, you can decide based on what you have seen and heard whether you want to purchase additional praise and worship DVDs.

I have recommended 25 DVDs. I have listed the approximate running time for each video. I normally plan on an hour and a half to two hours for an evening of watching praise and worship videos. Sometimes I combine two shorter videos if one video is not long enough.

In this first section I list recommended Gaither videos. DVDs can be ordered from gaither.com or from websites such as amazon.com, alibris.com and ebay.com.

1. *Because He Lives* – 115 minutes

This is an excellent DVD to watch first. This video gives you an overview of all Gaither videos. It contains early songs from the Gaither Trio and scenes from many Homecoming concerts. The story behind the Gaither videos is explained in this DVD.

2. *Jerusalem* – 100 minutes

I look for the purity of worship above all else when I recommend Christian worship DVDs. This book is about entering into the presence of God. The DVDs that I recommend contain songs that are very reverent. Many of the songs in this video are sung on the Sea of Galilee, the Mount of Olives and other historical places in the Holy Land.

3. *Israel Homecoming* – 105 minutes

This video also is very reverent. It contains reverent music from the Mount of Olives, the shore of the Jordan River, the Mount of Beatitudes, the Garden of Gethsemane and the Garden Tomb.

4. *A Billy Graham Music Homecoming* – 100 minutes

This video is very reverent. On many occasions singers can be seen wiping tears from their eyes. I believe that watching and participating in this DVD will help you to enter into the presence of God.

5. *The Gospel Music of the Statler Brothers, Volume 1* – 90 minutes

This video consists of interviews where Bill Gaither interviewed the members of this group approximately 10 years after they retired. Their comments are interspersed between the 19 recorded songs on this video. These men are very humble. Their songs are encouraging and uplifting. The song, *The Other Side of the Cross*, is particularly reverent.

6. *The Gospel Music of the Statler Brothers, Volume 2* – 90 minutes

This video also is excellent. The members of the Statler Brothers quartet have great integrity and servants' hearts. This video contains some fun entertainment, but it also contains a great deal of reverent worship music. If you like these two videos as much as Judy and I do, you will watch them again and again.

7. *Dottie Rambo with the Homecoming Friends* – 85 minutes

Dottie Rambo has written more than 2,500 songs. This outstanding video features 15 of her most-loved songs. Dottie's song, *He Looked Beyond My Faults*, is an outstanding worship song. Her song, *One More Valley*, is a triumphant song. *Sheltered in the Arms of God* is very encouraging. The closing song titled *We Shall Behold Him* sung by Sandi Patty is reverent and beautiful.

8. *The Best of the Booth Brothers* – 95 minutes

This video consists of an interview between Bill Gaither and the members of this trio – Ronnie Booth, Michael Booth and Jim Brady. Between songs they discuss their music and their lives. This video is filled with wonderful worship music and personal testimony from these three humble and sincere Christian men.

9. *Heaven* – 90 minutes

This video is very encouraging and uplifting. It contains at least 40 short comments from people giving their perspective on heaven. These comments are woven into more than 20 songs pertaining to heaven. This unique video will give you a glorious eternal perspective.

10. *Going Home* – 90 minutes

This video is a companion to *Heaven*. It was recorded by the same people in the same setting. It also contains approximately 40 short testimonies from people talking about heaven interspersed with 21 songs about heaven.

11. *The Journey to the Sky* – 105 minutes

This video contains worship songs from many Christian artists. The highlight of this video is Don Francisco singing his great song, *He is Alive*. The atmosphere is electric throughout this song. The audience erupts when he comes to the end.

12. *The Cathedrals – A Farewell Celebration* – 115 minutes

The Cathedrals have long been recognized as one of the greatest gospel quartets of all time. This video, which was made shortly before their retirement, culminated their 40-year career. This poignant farewell celebration is filled with nostalgic memories and reverent songs of praise.

13. *The Gatlin Brothers Come Home* – 80 minutes

This video explains how the Gatlin Brothers, Larry in particular, turned from their gospel roots to go into the world away from Christ. The opening song, *The Prodigal Son*, perfectly describes what happened to Larry as he came back to his Christian roots. Calvin

Newton sings *Wasted Years* to explain how he turned away from gospel music and went to prison. This video is an excellent story of coming back to Christ combined with excellent Christian music.

Carroll Roberson (carrollroberson.com)

On the remaining videos I will comment generally on the person or persons making the videos, not on the individual videos that I recommend.

If I had to choose one Christian musician who is *the most reverent* of any Christian musician I have ever watched, I would recommend Carroll Roberson. This man is a humble servant of God who reveres God. His reverence is seen throughout his videos. Carroll's songs are encouraging and uplifting. I often watch two of his videos in one night for a wonderful worship experience.

Carroll is joined on several videos by his wife, Donna, as they sing together. Donna's voice has operatic quality. I recommend that you try at least one of these videos to see for yourself the glorious worship experience in these videos. I believe that you then will be highly motivated to purchase additional videos.

Unlike some Christian artists, Carroll Roberson does not sing primarily to entertain. When you watch a Carroll Roberson video, you will know that he is not singing to entertain you. He sings to worship God. Carroll is sincere, humble and filled with gratitude. The photography of scenic areas on many of these videos is spectacular.

14. *God Made the Mountains* – 55 minutes
15. *Classic Gospel* – 45 minutes

16. *More Than a Man* – 50 minutes

17. *The Spirit of Praise* – 65 minutes

The Collingsworth Family (thecollingsworthfamily.com)

We have enjoyed the Collingsworth family since their children were very young. Three of the four children are now married. This inspiring family works together in magnificent worship to God.

18. *Hymns from Home*

This is the latest video by this wonderful Christian family at the time this book is written. This video consists of the family singing beautiful worship music from their home.

19. *A Decade of Memories*

This is a ten-year summary of this Christian family and the worship videos they have made. You will see the children grow into anointed and very talented young adults. The music in all Collingsworth Family videos is reverent and encouraging.

The Booth Brothers (boothbrothers.com)

20. *An Evening with the Booth Brothers* – 80 minutes

21. *The Booth Brothers in Louisville* – 100 minutes

We already have discussed the Booth Brothers on the summary of the Gaither videos. This trio has been a leading Christian music group for many years. As the years have gone by, they have become increasingly popular.

The Chuck Wagon Gang
(thechuckwagongang.net)

The Chuck Wagon Gang is a unique group. This quartet sings with a guitar and no other musical accompaniment. The original members of the Chuck Wagon Gang made their first recording in 1936. For many years they were the largest Christian recording group in the days of 78 rpm records. Their original small-town Americana singing style is carried forth to the present. The harmony is excellent and tightly knit.

Their recordings are reverent and low-key. They sing praise to God with simplicity and close harmony. There is none of the showmanship that is prevalent in some Christian videos. The old-fashioned singing style of this group continually glorifies Jesus Christ. Watching their videos is a unique and pleasant experience.

22. *Wagon Tracks Live* – 40 minutes

23. *Live at Renfro Valley* – 55 minutes

24. *Live at Branson* – 70 minutes

Grand Ole Gospel Reunion
(grandolegospelreunion.com)

I have a large collection of Grand Ole Gospel Reunion videos. The Grand Ole Gospel Reunion consists of many singing groups of the past who are semi-retired plus some active groups all coming together for an annual reunion. Some of the recordings are "good old boys" getting back together for some fun as opposed to reverent awe of God.

25. *The Grand Ole Gospel Reunion 2003 –
#2 of 3 – 120 minutes*

I have chosen DVD #2 of the 2003 Reunion as the most reverent recording I have seen from the Grand Ole Gospel Reunion. This video consists of three DVDs and must be ordered as a set. The price is a bargain at $25 for all three videos.

The first two videos, including the one that I recommend, are two hours in length. The third video is 95 minutes. You might want to check out this video because it is especially reverent. Any Christian who watches this outstanding video will have a wonderful worship experience.

If you like the Grand Ole Gospel Reunion videos, you will be able to choose from their large selection of DVDs from 1989 through 2006 when they stopped making videos. I have spent many enjoyable hours watching Grand Ole Gospel Reunion videos.

If you choose to order any of the DVDs that I recommend, I believe you will be very pleased with the video you receive. I have spent more than 4,000 evenings watching Christian DVDs and other Christian worship videos. The cumulative effect of these videos definitely has helped me to come more and more into the presence of God.

I am very grateful for my Christian worship video collection. I hope that you will try at least some of these recommended videos to see for yourself whether they will help you to come into the presence of God.

Chapter 14

Are You Living in the Presence of God?

In the introduction of this book we studied Psalm 105:4 where you are instructed to seek to be in God's presence *continually*. The holy Scriptures would not have told you to seek God's presence continually if it were not possible for you to live continually in God's presence.

There is *no* better place for any of us to be than in the presence of God. In Chapter 1 we studied Psalm 12:11 where you are told that fullness of joy is available to you when you are in God's presence. Think of the importance of these words. The words "fullness of joy" mean *all* of the joy there is. If you learn how to live in God's presence continually, you will experience *fullness* of joy continually.

In addition to experiencing fullness of joy from dwelling in God's presence, Psalm 91 tells us of the supernatural protection that you will receive when you are in God's presence. Psalm 91:7 says that, when you are in the secret place of the Most High, thousands will fall at your side and ten thousand will fall at your right hand but it shall *not* come near you. The supernatural protection that is available to you when you are in God's presence is amazing.

We know that, when Psalm 91:7 refers to the secret place of the Most High, it refers to God's presence. Psalm 31:20 refers to "the secret place of God's presence." Psalm 91:8-10 tell you that, when you dwell in the secret place of the Most High, no evil shall befall you and no calamity can come near you.

What could be more important than to learn how to live continually in God's presence and to experience fullness of joy at all times and to be totally protected at all times? In this chapter we will review the Scripture references that are used in this book. If you accurately complete the following questionnaire, you will be able to *clearly identify* any changes that you will need to make so that you will live continually in God's presence.

We are using this format rather than the Study Guide that we normally use at the end of our books. We are doing this because we want to place together in one chapter a way for you to clearly identify exactly what you should do to live continually in the presence of God.

Questions to Ask Yourself

1. Are you in *absolute awe* of the opportunity that you have been given to live continually in the presence of God? (see Psalm 105:4, I Chronicles 16:11, Psalm 27:8, Psalm 68:8 and Psalm 114:7 in Chapter 1) .... Yes ___ No ___

2. Are you doing your best to consistently turn *away* from the superficial ways of the world so that you will be able to live continually in God's presence? (see Philippians 3:20, I Peter 2:11, Romans 12:2 and I Timothy 6:20 in Chapter 2) .... Yes ___ No ___

3. Is Jesus Christ truly in *first* place in your life ahead of everyone and everything else? (see Colossians 1:18, John 3:30, I John 2:27 and Psalm 73:25 in Chapter 2) .... Yes ___ No ___

4. Do you fear and revere God and hold Him in constant awe? (see Ecclesiastes 12:13, Jeremiah 32:40, Psalm 25:14, I Peter 1:17, Proverbs 23:17 and II Corinthians 7:1 in Chapter 3) .... Yes ___ No ___

5. Is your relationship with God more intimate than it was a year ago? Are you constantly drawing closer to God? (see I John 5:20, Ephesians 2:13, Philippians 3:10-11, I Chronicles 22:19, Psalm 42:2, Psalm 63:1, Hosea 6:3, Jeremiah 29:13, Hebrews 12:14, James 4:8 and Romans 6:11 in Chapter 3) .... Yes ___ No ___

6. Do you have a continual consciousness that God lives in your heart? Does your life revolve around your absolute certainty of His indwelling presence? (see Ephesians 4:6, Ephesians 3:17, I Corinthians 3:16, Colossians 2:10 and Acts 17:27-28 in Chapter 4) .... Yes ___ No ___

7. Have you entered into God's rest so that you are able to face adversity because you are resting in God with complete confidence in Him? (see Exodus 33:14, Hosea 14:3, Hebrews 4:10 and II Timothy 4:5 in Chapter 4)
.... Yes ___ No ___

8. Are you living with absolute assurance that God is supernaturally protecting you because you are in His presence? (see Proverbs 29:5, Psalm 91:1, Psalm 31:20, Psalm 91:2, Psalm 91:7-10, Psalm 9:9 and Psalm 57:1 in Chapter 4)
.... Yes ___ No ___

9. Are you proud and self-centered? Do you understand that people who are proud often block themselves from intimacy with God? (see Philippians 2:21, Isaiah 14:12-14, Revelation 12:9 and I Peter 5:5 in Chapter 5)
.... Yes ___ No ___

10. Are you truly a humble person? Does your lifestyle place God first, other people second and yourself last? (see I Peter 5:5, Psalm 138:6, Luke 14:11, Matthew 11:29, John 5:41, Philippians 2:5, Proverbs 3:34, Proverbs 14:6, Psalm 25:9 and James 3:13 in Chapter 5)
.... Yes ___ No ___

11. Jesus Christ died so that you would live for Him instead of living for yourself. Do you consistently surrender control of your life to the Holy Spirit? (II Corinthians 5:15, Acts 16:31, Proverbs 16:9, Galatians 2:20, Matthew 10:39, Romans 6:13, Isaiah 64:8, Romans 8:4,

Romans 8:9, Galatians 5:16, Galatians 5:25 and I Thessalonians 5:16 in Chapter 6) .... Yes ___ No ___

12. Are you so grateful to God and to Jesus Christ that your heart overflows with gratitude? Is your heart so full of gratitude that you thank God and thank Jesus on many occasions during each day of your life? (see John 3:16, Philippians 2:6-8, Mark 14:35-36, Isaiah 52:14, Luke 23:33, Matthew 27:46 and II Corinthians 5:21 in Chapter 7).......................... Yes ___ No ___

13. The Bible teaches that we come into God's presence by thanking Him continually. Do you thank God many times each day? (see Psalm 95:2, Psalm 100:4, II Corinthians 9:15, Psalm 136:1-3, I Thessalonians 2:13, II Peter 1:4, I Thessalonians 5:18, Psalm 116:17, II Corinthians 2:14, John 16:33, I John 5:4-5, Romans 8:37-39 and Philippians 4:6-7 in Chapter 8) .... Yes ___ No ___

14. The Bible teaches that continually praising God brings you into His presence. Are you continually praising God because of your awe of Who He is and your gratitude for everything He does for you? (see Psalm 22:3, Isaiah 43:21, Psalm 145:3, Psalm 150:2, Psalm 22:23, Psalm 67:3, Psalm 67:5, Psalm 113:3, Psalm 71:8, Matthew 12:34, Psalm 34:1, Hebrews 13:15, Psalm 134:2, Psalm 71:5-6, Psalm 56:10-11, Isaiah 66:2, Romans 4:20, Isaiah 61:3 and Proverbs 27:21 in Chapter 9) .... Yes ___ No ___

15. The Bible repeatedly emphasizes the importance of singing praise to God. Do you continually sing praises to God? Do you often sing praises to Him with musical accompaniment? (see Psalm 100:1-2, Psalm 84:4, Psalm 66:1-2, Psalm 61:8, Psalm 92:4, Psalm 135:3, Psalm 13:5-6, Psalm 28:7, Psalm 57:7, Acts 16:22-26, II Chronicles 20:12-22, Psalm 69:29-30, James 5:13, Psalm 98:4, Psalm 47:6-7, Ephesians 5:18-20, Psalm 92:1, Psalm 98:5-6 and Psalm 150:3-5 in Chapters 10 and 11) .... Yes __ No __

If you have answered each of the 15 questions in this chapter affirmatively, you *are* living in the glorious presence of God. If you answered some of these questions affirmatively and some negatively, you have a clear indication of the changes that God desires you to make in your life so that you will dwell in His presence.

Conclusion

This book is filled with God's instructions pertaining to entering into His presence. There is no greater experience this side of heaven than to continually live in the presence of God during our lives on earth.

Please pray about sharing a copy of this book with your friends and loved ones. Living in the presence of God is the greatest experience that Christians can enjoy on earth. Every person who has received Jesus Christ as his or her Savior will live eternally in the presence of God in heaven. We believe that sharing this book with other Christians will enable these people to partake of the awesome experience of living in God's presence during their lives on earth.

In order to enable you to purchase several copies of our publications, we provide a 40% discount for 5-9 items and a 50% discount for any 10 or more items. From our beginning God has instructed us to give our readers similar discounts to the discounts that bookstores receive when they purchase books in quantity. See the order form at the back of this book.

If this book has helped you, would you share your testimony with us so that we can share with others what God has done in your life through *Live Continually in the Presence of God*? We normally need three to four paragraphs in a testimony so that we can consolidate this information into one solid paragraph for our newsletter and our website. Your comments will encourage many people, including pastors and leaders in Third World countries and inmates in prisons and jails who receive our books free of charge.

Please send any comments that you have to us at lamplightmin@yahoo.com. You can call 1-800-540-1597 and leave a message for Judy. You also can mail your comments to Lamplight Ministries, Inc., PO Box 1307, Dunedin, FL 34697.

We invite you to visit our website at www.lamplight.net. You will find many comments from people who have been helped by our books, Scripture cards and CDs. You also will find a section on biblical health as well as recipes that Judy adds each month to bless you. We are in good health at ages 83 and 75. I know that I would not be alive today if it were not for Judy's knowledge and wisdom regarding health and her amazing recipes.

You can keep in touch with us on Facebook (facebook.com/jackandjudylamplight) and Twitter (twitter.com/lamplightmin). You can follow our blog at lamplightmin.wordpress.com You can receive frequent updates on our latest books. You can order our books as e-books at SmashWords.com – enter "Jack Hartman."

We ask you to pray for us. We are completing two books each year with no foreseeable plans to stop delivering God's Word to readers with a simple and easy-to-understand explanation. Your prayers for us will make a difference.

We have been blessed to share with you the results of hundreds of hours that we have invested to explain what the Word of God teaches about living in the presence of God during your life on earth. We will be excited to hear about your journey with Jesus Christ through this book. We are looking forward to hearing from you.

Blessed to be a blessing. (Genesis 12:1-3)

Jack and Judy

Appendix

Trusting in Jesus Christ as Your Savior

This book is filled with instructions and promises from God. If you have not received Jesus Christ as your Savior, you very likely cannot understand the scriptural truths that are contained in this book. "...the mind of the flesh [with its carnal thoughts and purposes] is hostile to God, for it does not submit itself to God's Law; indeed it cannot." (Romans 8:7)

Many people who have not received Jesus Christ as their Savior are not open to the specific instructions that God has given to us in the Bible. "...the natural, nonspiritual man does not accept or welcome or admit into his heart the gifts and teachings and revelations of the Spirit of God, for they are folly (meaningless nonsense) to him; and he is incapable of knowing them [of progressively recognizing, understanding, and becoming better acquainted with them] because they are spiritually discerned and estimated and appreciated." (I Corinthians 2:14)

The words "does not accept or welcome or admit into his heart the gifts and teachings and revelations of the Spirit of God" in this verse of Scripture are very important. Some people are opposed to the Bible and what it teaches. They look at Scripture references from the Bible as "meaningless nonsense." These people block themselves from learning great scriptural truths from God. Their hearts must be softened. Their spirits must be quickened by the Holy Spirit of God through Jesus Christ.

At the close of this Appendix we will explain exactly what God instructs you to do to receive Jesus Christ as your Savior. When you make this decision, the glorious supernatural truths of the Bible will come alive to you. Jesus said, "...To you it has been given to know the secrets and mysteries of the kingdom of heaven, but to them it has not been given." (Matthew 13:11)

These words that Jesus spoke to His disciples many years ago also are His words to you when He said that *you* can "know the secrets and mysteries of the kingdom of heaven." Do not miss out on the glorious privilege that is available to every believer to know and understand the ways of God.

A spiritual veil blocks all unbelievers from understanding scriptural truths. "...even if our Gospel (the glad tidings) also be hidden (obscured and covered up with a veil that hinders the knowledge of God), it is hidden [only] to those who are perishing and obscured [only] to those who are spiritually dying and veiled [only] to those who are lost." (II Corinthians 4:3)

This spiritual veil is pulled aside when you receive Jesus Christ as your Savior. "...whenever a person turns [in repentance] to the Lord, the veil is stripped off and taken away." (II Corinthians 3:16)

If you obey the scriptural instructions at the end of this Appendix, Jesus Christ will become your Savior. Everything in your life will become fresh and new. "...if any person is [ingrafted] in Christ (the Messiah) he is a new creation (a new creature altogether); the old [previous moral and spiritual condition] has passed away. Behold, the fresh and new has come!" (II Corinthians 5:17)

Instead of being opposed to the teachings of the holy Bible, you will be completely open to these teachings. You will have a hunger and thirst to continually learn more supernatural truths from the holy Scriptures. "...I endorse and delight in the Law of God in my inmost self [with my new nature]." (Romans 7:22)

Every person who has not received Jesus Christ as his or her Savior is a sinner who is doomed to live throughout eternity in the horror of hell. God has made it possible for you to escape this terrible eternal penalty. "...God so greatly loved and dearly prized the world that He [even] gave up His only begotten (unique) Son, so that whoever believes in (trusts in, clings to, relies on) Him shall not perish (come to destruction, be lost) but have eternal (everlasting) life." (John 3:16)

God knew that everyone who lived on earth after Adam and Eve would be a sinner because of the sin nature they inherited from Adam and Eve (see Romans 3:10-12). Therefore, to re-establish the personal communication God had with Adam and Eve, He sent His only Son to take upon Himself the sins of the world as He gave up His life on the cross. If you believe that Jesus Christ paid the full price for *your* sins and if you trust Him completely for your eternal salvation, you will live with Him eternally in the glory of heaven. Then you will want to shout the glorious news to everyone you meet.

There is only *one* way for you to live eternally in heaven after you die – that is to receive eternal salvation through Jesus Christ. "Jesus said to him, I am the Way and the Truth and the Life; no one comes to the Father except by (through) Me." (John 14:6)

If you trust in anyone or anything except Jesus Christ for your eternal salvation, you will not live eternally in heaven. If you are reading these truths about living eternally in heaven because of the price that Jesus Christ has paid for you, you can be certain that the same God Who created you actually is drawing you to come to Jesus Christ for eternal salvation. Jesus said, "No one is able to come to Me unless the Father Who sent Me attracts and draws him and gives him the desire to come to Me..." (John 6:44)

Are you interested in these spiritual truths about where you will live throughout eternity? If you are, you can be certain that the same awesome God Who created you is *drawing you* to Jesus Christ. You will enter the kingdom of God through Jesus Christ. You actually will begin eternal life in Christ Jesus the moment you believe in Him (see Romans 6:23).

Heaven is a glorious place. Everyone in heaven is completely healthy and full of joy. "God will wipe away every tear from their eyes; and death shall be no more, neither shall there be anguish (sorrow and mourning) nor grief nor pain any more, for the old conditions and the former order of things have passed away." (Revelation 21:4)

All of the problems of life on earth will disappear when you arrive in heaven. No one in heaven dies. No one in heaven is sad. No one in heaven cries. No one in heaven suffers from pain.

You *will* live throughout eternity in one place or another. If you do not receive Jesus Christ as your Savior, you will live eternally in hell. People in hell will experience continual torment throughout eternity. "...the smoke of their torment ascends forever and ever; and they have no respite (no pause, no intermission, no rest, no peace) day or night..." (Revelation 14:11)

Everyone in heaven is filled with joy. Everyone in hell is miserable. Jesus described what hell would be like when He said, "...there will be weeping and wailing and grinding of teeth. (Matthew 13:42)

Throughout eternity the inhabitants of hell will weep and wail. They will grind their teeth in anguish. Can you imagine living this way for the endless trillions of years of eternity? This is exactly what will happen if you *reject* the supreme sacrifice that Jesus Christ made to pay the full price for your sins.

How do you receive eternal salvation through Jesus Christ? "...if you acknowledge and confess with your lips that Jesus is Lord and in your heart believe (adhere to, trust in, and rely on the truth) that God raised Him from the dead, you will be saved. For with the heart a person believes (adheres to, trusts in, and relies on Christ) and so is justified (declared righteous, acceptable to God), and with the mouth he confesses (declares openly and speaks out freely his faith) and confirms [his] salvation." (Romans 10:9-10)

Repent of your sins. You must *believe in your heart* (not just think in your mind) that Jesus Christ paid the full price for all of your sins when He was crucified. You must believe that God actually raised Jesus from the dead. You must open your mouth and *speak* this truth that you believe in your heart. If you believe in your heart that Jesus Christ died and rose again from the dead and that the price for your sins has been paid for and you tell others that you believe this great spiritual truth, you *have* been saved. You *will* live eternally in heaven.

If Jesus Christ was not your Savior when you began to read this book, we pray that He is your Savior now. Your life will change immensely. You will never be the same again. Every aspect of your life will be gloriously new.

If you have become a child of God by receiving eternal salvation through Jesus Christ, we welcome you to the family of God. Please let us know that you have made this wonderful decision by contacting us at lamplightmin@yahoo.com, 1-800-540-1497 or PO Box 1307, Dunedin, FL 34697. We would like to pray for you and welcome you as our new Christian brother or sister. We love you and bless you in the name of our Lord Jesus Christ.

We would be so pleased to hear from you. If you are already a believer, we would be pleased to hear from you as well. We invite you to visit our website at www.lamplight.net. Please let us know if this book or one or more of our other publications has made a difference in your life. Please give us your comments so that we can share these comments in our newsletters and on our website to encourage other people.

A Few Words About Lamplight Ministries

Lamplight Ministries, Inc. originally began in 1983 as Lamplight Publications. After ten years as a publishing firm with a goal of selling Christian books, Lamplight Ministries was established in 1991. Jack and Judy Hartman founded Lamplight Ministries with a mission of continuing to sell their publications and also to *give* large numbers of these publications free of charge to needy people all over the world.

Lamplight Ministries was created to allow people who have been blessed by our publications to share in financing the translation, printing and distribution of our books into other languages and also to distribute our publications free of charge to inmates in jails and prisons. Over the years many partners of Lamplight Ministries have shared Jack and Judy's vision. Thousands of people in jails and prisons and in Third World countries have received our publications free of charge.

Our books and Scripture Meditation Cards have been translated into eleven foreign languages – Armenian, Danish, Greek, Hebrew, German, Korean, Norwegian, Portuguese, Russian, Spanish and the Tamil dialect in India. The translations in these languages are not available from Lamplight Ministries in the United States. These translations can only be obtained in the countries where we have given permission for them to be published.

The pastors of many churches in Third World countries have written to say that they consistently preach sermons in their churches based on the scriptural contents of our publications. We believe that people in several churches in *many* different countries hear sermons that are based on the scriptural contents of our publications. Praise the Lord!

Jack Hartman was the sole author of twelve Christian books. After co-authoring one book with Judy, Jack and Judy co-authored ten sets of Scripture Meditation Cards. Judy has been the co-author of every subsequent book. Jack and Judy currently are working on other books that they believe the Lord is leading them to write as co-authors.

We invite you to request our newsletters to stay in touch with us, to learn of our latest publications and to read comments from people all over the world. Please write, fax, call or email us. You are very special to us. We love you and thank God for you. Our heart is to take the gospel to the world and for our books to be available in every known language. Hallelujah!

Lamplight Ministries, Inc.,
PO Box 1307 - Dunedin, Florida, 34697. USA
Phone: 1-800-540-1597
Fax: 1-727-784-2980
website: lamplight.net
email: lamplightmin@yahoo.com

Enthusiastic Comments from Readers of Our Publications

The following are just a few of the many comments we have received from people in *61 countries* pertaining to our publications. For additional comments, see our website: lamplight.net.

Trust God for Your Finances

There are more than 150,000 copies of *Trust God for Your Finances* in print. This book has been translated into seven foreign languages.

- "I have translated *Trust God for Your Finances* into Thai. I intended to make about 50 or 60 photocopies of this translation to distribute among friends. My pastor asked for 700 copies to distribute at the special yearly conference for pastors. My immediate thought was that I could not do this, but he urged me to pray and try my best. Surprisingly, it worked out. Thank God. More than 1,000 people attended the conference. Seven hundred copies were distributed to only the pastors, elders and deacons who really wanted the book. After the conference, we had so many calls that another 2,000 copies were printed. Thank you, Mr. Hartman, for this book which is helping so many Thai Christians." (Thailand)

- "I bought your book, *Trust God for Your Finances*, at a church I was attending in Virginia in the 1980s. This book transformed my life. It was all Bible-based and solid in every way. I married a Bulgarian pastor who started the church here during Communism and the underground church. We have pastored together for 22 years. I gave your book to my husband and he consumed it. He kept it near his Bible all the time. God has raised him up to be influential in this nation. He has written a book titled *The Covenant of Provision* dealing with finances. Your book helped him so much to form his ideas about the rightful use of money. This book has influenced my husband more than almost any other book. It was so timely and needed coming out of a Communist society. Thank you so much for this book." (Bulgaria)

- "Today we had a ministry partner join us for lunch. He said that the book, *Trust God for Your Finances*, that we had translated into Hebrew was the most powerful book he had ever read on the subject. I shared with him the wonderful story of how you shared the book with us and how many Israelis have been enlightened in that area as a result of reading the book. You both are a blessing and a treasure in God's kingdom." (Israel)

What Does God Say?

- "Your book *What Does God Say?* is one of the greatest books I have ever read. You tell the truth and back it up with Scripture. I started crime very young. I have spent a large portion of my life behind bars. I have so much to be ashamed of and things that I am very sorry for. I have almost wasted my life. I say almost because this book caused me to realize that God loves even me no matter what I have done. In your book I read that there is no condemnation in Christ Jesus. Do you have any idea what it means to feel no condemnation when society says to lock me up because I am guilty? My sins and all the crimes I have committed have been washed away. I cannot explain how it feels to know that someone is really proud of me. That someone is Jesus. I am taking this book home with me. Even though I don't have much education, I can understand it very well. I now know that I am saved and I am forgiven. Thank you very much for writing this book." (Florida)

- "Several months ago, you sent me a copy of your book titled *What Does God Say?*. This book is amazing. First of all, I could understand it. My English is not great. I have been a Muslim all my life. I was taught as a child what I was supposed to believe. When I was searching for real truth, I met the Master and received Jesus Christ as my Savior. When I read your book, it filled so much of the void and loneliness that I was filled with. I will be sharing Jesus and *What Does God Say?* with my family and with other Muslims. Please pray for me as I may not be welcomed in my own home town for finding this wonderful Jesus." (Ghana)

- "Our ministry here in South Africa is flourishing. We thank God for the books from Jack and Judy

Hartman. The book, *What Does God Say?*, is my daily manual. It addresses all issues of life. I read it every day and I love it. I am complete. This book has made our ministry more effective. I no longer have to struggle on what to preach or teach. I am now equipped with the correct material. This book is filled with the anointing and revelation of God. My fellow pastors here in South Africa are hungry for these books. We soon will be opening a branch in Pretoria and also in Botswana. I thank God for the Hartmans. I always pray for them." (South Africa)

Quiet Confidence in the Lord

- "As soon as I was diagnosed with prostate cancer, I began to meditate on the Scripture and your explanation of the Scripture in *Quiet Confidence in the Lord*. I carried this book with me everywhere for several weeks. The specialist at the Lahey Clinic in Boston told me I was the calmest person with this diagnosis that he had ever seen. During the pre-op and the surgery, a number of people commented on how calm I was. I experienced a lot of discomfort during the difficult first week at home after the surgery. I focused constantly on the Scripture in this wonderful book. I was remarkably calm. Thank you for writing this book that has helped me so much." (Massachusetts)

- "After I graduated from Bible school, I went outside of my country for mission work with my wife. After we were there for nine months, my wife died suddenly. My sorrow was great. I read your book titled *Quiet Confidence in the Lord*. This book spoke to my heart. All twenty-three chapters were written for me. God changed me through this book and comforted me and took away my sorrow. Through the blood of Jesus I entered God's rest. I can give a great recommendation for this book to anyone who is filled with sorrow and grief. I pray that many people will read this book and develop quiet confidence in the Lord as I did. Thank you so much for sending this book to me. May God bless you and your ministry." (Ethiopia)

- "*Quiet Confidence in the Lord* is with me at work each day. I have read and underlined passages that lift my heart and help me to understand something I've known all along and that is that I am not alone and that God cares very much that I'm in the midst of great adversity. I asked God to send me a comforter, someone who would put their arms around me and say, 'I understand and I care.' The answer to that prayer is in you and Judy. Thanks to *Quiet Confidence of the Lord* I am, for the first time in my life, learning to focus on God and not my problems. Thank you both for your ministry. Your books are a tremendous blessing to hurting people all over the world." (Washington, DC)

God's Instructions for Growing Older

- "I am a 63-year-old businesswoman from Thailand. Like most women around the world, I do not like growing old. When I received a copy of your book, *God's Instructions For Growing Older*, I read straight from the first page to the last in two days. Your book gives me the assurance of how to grow older without fear, anxiety, and worry. I will live the rest of my life in peace and joy for I now know that if we keep God in first place at all times, the final years of our lives will be meaningful, productive, and fulfilling. Thank you, Mr. and Mrs. Hartman, for the priceless gift of your book. May God bless you and your team always." (Thailand)

- "I have never read a book like *God's Instructions for Growing Older*. Finally a book has been written that teaches how to finish our course in life as a Christian. Your chapter on Scripture meditation is pure gold. This book is a road map to direct us in the way the Lord intends for us to grow older. Thank you so much for this special book." (Florida)

- "Thank you for your new book, *God's Instructions for Growing Older*. I love this book. I read a little bit every day so that I can be an encourager to my older friends and to myself. We so need God's knowledge during the final years of our lives. I have started my gift list to share this book with others." (Texas)

Receive Healing from the Lord

- "Your great book, *Receive Healing from the Lord*, has amazed me. This book has been my daily bread. I have followed all of God's instructions in your book. My children and my wife were healed from severe illness. I was sick myself just before an important crusade. I meditated on the Scripture in your book for the entire night. I was totally healed. The following day God did wonders as He healed many people. Since then, people have been coming to receive their healing at our home and church almost every day. Many healings are taking place at our services. This book is wonderful. I am abundantly blessed by it." (Zambia)

- "My husband and I served in the mission field in Swaziland, Africa, for three and a half years. Upon our arrival, Lamplight Ministries sent us four mailbags full of Jack and Judy's books. Because Swaziland is so laden with HIV/AIDS, we were able to use the book, *Receive Healing from the Lord*, with the people in Swaziland to see many people come to a saving knowledge of the Lord Jesus Christ and His perfect will regarding healing. We saw mothers with very sick children who themselves also were afflicted with AIDS respond to the many Scriptures that are part of the book, actually believing that it was meant for them. Had it not been for the use of this book and the other books you sent, we would not have had such success in teaching a Bible study about the truth in God's Word to these people. We gave out your books and told the people that the book was theirs to keep. We saw such joy and surprise on the faces of these impoverished people. We appreciate the ongoing generosity of Lamplight Ministries for 'such a time as this' in these days where there is so much need and want. We will forever be thankful that we can count on the Word of God through the books written by Jack and Judy as effective tools in the transformation of people's lives." (Swaziland)

- "Thank you very much for sending me your book, *Receive Healing from the Lord*. After reading the first chapter I realized that this book could be the solution for my wife's failing health. We decided to read the book together every day. My wife was healed and restored after carefully following the scriptural principles that you explained. We are humbled by how we had struggled and panicked trying to find an answer. God gave us the solution in your book. We are so grateful to you. We love you and we are praying for you." (Zambia)

You Can Hear the Voice of God

- "Many years of my life I scoffed at Christians. I looked at them as holy rollers. When I was incarcerated, I experienced pain as I have never felt in my life. A darkness and loneliness like I have never experienced before came upon me. A friend here gave me your book, *You Can Hear the Voice of God*. If there ever was a time when I needed to hear from God, it is now. My wife was desperately ill at the very point of death when I started reading your book. I now know that God has been trying to talk to me all of my life, but I didn't know how to listen to His voice. NOW I CAN HEAR THE VOICE OF GOD. In a splendid and simple way you actually taught me how to hear the voice of God Almighty. How can I ever thank you? Thank you for writing this book. It will impact hundreds of thousands, I am sure." (Florida)

- "Thank you for sending me a copy of *You Can Hear the Voice of God*. This book is so good. On the first day of having this book in my hands, I read continually. I finished five chapters. My wife was invited to teach at a meeting of pastors' wives. The women were excited because of this teaching. I would like to translate this book into Benba, one of the largest spoken languages on the copper belt and some provinces of Zambia. Would you give me permission to translate this book? I know that the Holy Spirit has inspired me to do so." (Zambia) (Permission was granted.)

- "Thank you for the box of books that you sent to a pastor who is a friend of mine. He gave me a copy of your book *You Can Hear The Voice of God*. This book is a spiritual manual for the serious Christian. I thank God for Jack and Judy Hartman. This book is helping me to draw closer to my Maker. I now realize that God has been talking to me daily but I did not hear Him. This book is a real blessing to the body of Christ." (Ghana)

Effective Prayer

- "I thank God for your book titled *Effective Prayer*. This book came to me at the right time. Since reading this book, God has done great wonders in my life and ministry. Our whole church is being affected by what we have learned about the power of prayer. I have read many books on prayer, but this one is unique. I no longer pray amiss. My prayer life has become much more effective. Your book has helped me to persevere in prayer much longer than before. This is a great book. I love it. I treasure this book. I do not know how to thank you. I pray that God will bless you both with long life and that you will enjoy the fruit of your labour." (Zambia)

- "Your book *Effective Prayer* is a great blessing to me. After reading this book I have so much more understanding about prayer. It is very easy to learn from all that you are teaching and all of the

Scriptures in it. I now understand much more about the significance of prayer in my daily life, why I should pray and how to pray. You have enlightened my mind. I know that my loving Father wants me to pray all the time. I have learned to pray God's answer instead of focusing on the problem. This book is very vital to my daily life. I am so thankful to both of you for another great book for people who need answers. Thank you so much for the great understanding that I found in this book." (the Philippines)

- "I have been studying your book *Effective Prayer*. This book has inspired me to do a lot more praying. Praying to God is such a privilege. To know that God is just waiting for me to come and talk with Him is tremendous. The way you brought out the gift of being baptized in the Holy Spirit and praying in tongues will make it easier for people to receive this much-needed gift in their lives. Our pastor is using your book to teach on prayer. I have given copies of this book to many people in our church. I gave one to another pastor in our town. I love you both in the Lord Jesus Christ. I thank God for you and for allowing Him to continue to use you in the body of Christ." (Oklahoma)

Never, Never Give Up

- "I am a 68-year-old businessman. At my age I should be enjoying a life way past retirement. It is not so. In 1997 Thailand suffered a severe economic crunch and my business almost went down under. It took me many years to try to come back. Just as I thought I was climbing out of the black hole, another crisis hit two years ago. This time I am too old to fight, but I have no choice but to go on. I thought that God and I were very close. However, after the first crisis hit I sort of lost my faith along with my hope. After the second crisis hit, I thought that God had forsaken me. I all but lost my faith totally until one day a good friend gave me a book, *Never, Never Give Up*. At first I didn't want to read it. However, insisted by my friend, I did. I stayed up the whole night finishing the book. By morning I kneeled down and begged God to forgive me for my foolishness. I felt so ashamed for my behavior. I begged Him to accept me back. After I did that, I know that God has forgiven me. Now I am back to feeling close to Him again. I am so happy and grateful for this book. God is great!" (Thailand)

- "Thanks for being there when you are so much needed by all of us. After seven major operations I am beginning to walk again and help others which is the full purpose of my existence which Jesus Christ has set before me. Your book, *Never, Never Give Up*, stayed by my pillow along with my Bible while I was recuperating from these operations. When I re-read it, I was charged with peace and energy again. The pain diminishes and I can speak of God's infinite love and mercy to others who are facing similar trials. Thank you for writing this God-inspired book." (Florida)

- "Suicide has shown its face in my mind. I found myself falling deeper and deeper into the pit of hell. My life seemed so grim. I could not see where I could make a difference and was planning to believe that if I chose to leave this life it would not matter. When I received *Never, Never Give Up* I read the first three chapters that evening. When I arrived at page ninety, your verse changed my life. I want you to know that I have been delivered from this season of trial. I rededicated my life to the Lord and feel wonderful. Thank you so much for your work. Through our Lord you have saved my life. Thank you for my life back." (Texas)

Reverent Awe of God

- "Greetings in the mighty name of our Lord Jesus. Thank you for sending me a free copy of *Reverent Awe of God*. I was surprised to learn your ages when I read this book. You are still relevant in your books. You are changing the destiny of many people globally. I will use this book to teach our church members from the many valuable lessons that I have learned from your book. May God bless you and supply all of your needs." (Kenya)

- "A student in one of the universities read your book, *Reverent Awe of God*, from our library. As a result, she was converted from the Muslim religion to Christianity. She said that the concept of our Christian faith is more real. She can see that God is her Father and that Jesus Christ is real and the only Son of God. This student said that she is facing attacks and rejections from her home. She needs our prayers. Papa, thank you." (Ghana)

- "We are very grateful for the box of books you sent us. I praise God for your new book, *Reverent Awe of God*. This book can really help any believer to establish a genuine relationship with our Maker. When we read your books and consider your age, we thank God that the Spirit of God never grows old. May God continue to bless you and give you long life so that you will write many more books that explain the Word of God to us." (Ghana)

Overcoming Fear

- "Thank you for sending your books to the Philippines. I was very blessed to read *Overcoming Fear*. This book explained the sources of fear and what I should do to overcome fear. It is really a blessing to know all of this information that helped me to overcome the fear I have felt all these years. I have cherished every chapter in the book. It has become food for my soul. Thank you so much for explaining all of this so well. I have learned that I should never be afraid of anyone because I can be absolutely certain that God lives in my heart. This is great assurance because I know that God is greater than anything I will ever face in this life. This book has been a great blessing in my life. God bless you both." (the Philippines)
- "I want to thank you immediately for your new book, *Overcoming Fear*. I have read every one of your books and given copies to many people, but I want to tell you that I believe this is your best book ever. I can hardly put it down. The day I received it I stayed up late, even though I was very tired, to read the first four chapters. The next morning I read two more chapters before going to work. This book is very inspiring. It gives me great peace. God's peace is so great that I cannot describe it. I have almost finished reading this book. When I am done, I will immediately read it again. Enclosed is a check for

ten copies of this book plus a contribution to Lamplight Ministries. Thank you, Jack and Judy, for writing this wonderful book." (Massachusetts)

- "I want to thank you for publishing the book *Overcoming Fear*. I am reading mine for the second time. I cannot tell you how comforting it is. The way you have put information along with the right Bible verses is so truly helpful. As world conditions worsen, I can tell you that this book will be a constant companion alongside my Bible. I am so grateful for you both. Keep up the good work. You are making a big difference in peoples' lives. You have in mine." (Minnesota)

Victory Over Adversity

- "I am a pure and proud Dutchman married to a Tanzanian woman. I have had a lot of problems staying with an African wife in Europe. I love my wife so much, but the environment for my wife was not good enough in terms of getting a job. This affected us very much to the extent that I was even planning to relocate to Tanzania for the sake of my wife and children's future. Thank God that an angel was sent to me by the name of Jim who gave me a book, *Victory over Adversity*. This book is amazing and great. It contains the answers to my problems and is a great encouragement to me. As a Dutchman I find it very interesting to read a book with simple English. Putting the facts of this book into practice has changed my life greatly. I have found a new job. My wife has found a good job. The thoughts of relocating to Tanzania have faded. My faith has increased and my commitment to God has grown. I pray that God will bless the writers of this book and also the man who gave me this book. My wife and I are always reading this book. It is our source of strength." (Holland)

- "I praise God for His living Word. Thank you for the books that you have sent to China. You cannot imagine what *Victory over Adversity* did in my life as a young believer. Not only is the language clear and accessible, but the content is very rewarding. I learned a lot from this book. I now meditate day and night on the Word of God. I am in the presence of God often. I am confident that I can overcome any adversity in the precious name of Jesus Christ. May God bless you and fill you with His infinite grace, Mr. Jack and his wife." (China)

- "I am a 22-year-old college student in Thailand. My family is half Christian. My mother is a Christian whereas my father is a Buddhist. I am the eldest daughter of my parents with one younger brother and sister. All three of us have been baptized as Christians since birth. Frankly, I have never had much faith in God and always have had problems with both of my parents. I think that they don't understand me. They think I don't listen to them. Last month my mother was given a book, *Victory over Adversity*, by her friend. Out of curiosity I took the book and read it before she did. I could not put it down. For the first time I felt that God is real and is close to me. I cried and cried and felt sorry for my past behavior toward God and my parents. I went to my mother and apologized, to her great surprise. Now I go to church with her every Sunday. I am very thankful to my mother's friend who gave her this book and also to the writers of this book who have changed my life and brought me to God which my mother could not do. Thank you both!" (Thailand)

Exchange Your Worries for God's Perfect Peace

- "*Exchange Your Worries for God's Perfect Peace* is a masterpiece. I am reading this book to the people here in the Philippines. I saw tears flowing down their faces as I read them parts of this book. I must get this book translated into their language. I am reading this book for the second time. After 30 years in the ministry I have finally learned how to turn my worries over to God. I have learned more from this book in the last few months than I have ever learned in my life. I will not allow my copy of this book to leave my presence. I thank God for you." (the Philippines)

- "I just want to tell you how much I appreciate you and your excellent book, *Exchange Your Worries for God's Perfect Peace*. I have read all of your books several times each. I continually go back to refer to the notes I have made in your books. I have done this for close to 15 years and pages are falling out of your books. I read the Bible daily. Your books are a close second to the Bible. I have never found another Christian author who teaches me more about God's Word and speaks directly to my heart as your writings do. Thank you for helping me appreciate and respect the Word of God." (Wisconsin)

- "I was in despair struggling with my life and ministry. *Exchange Your Worries for God's Perfect Peace* has strengthened me and encouraged my heart. My country is often threatened by disasters. Your book and the Scripture in it has helped me to focus on God, no matter what circumstances I have experienced and will face in the future. The language in the book is very clear and easy to understand for someone like me who uses English as a second language. I have been blessed by reading this book. My faith in Jesus has increased. Thank you for sending this book to me. I thank God that I know you. You are a blessing." (Indonesia)

God's Joy Regardless of Circumstances

- "*God's Joy Regardless of Circumstances* came to me right on time. Being in prison for 20 years for a crime I didn't commit and then having to deal with severe family problems is not a morsel that is easy to swallow. My oldest daughter was pregnant and we were looking forward to having my first grandson born. We were very pained to learn that my daughter had to lose her baby. In the midst of dealing with this problem, you sent me a free copy of *God's Joy Regardless of Circumstances*. When I avidly started to read this book, my daughter underwent surgery, lost her baby and faced uncertainty and despair. *God's Joy Regardless of Circumstances* pulled us through. Thank you also for sending a free copy of this book to my daughter. May God continue blessing Lamplight Ministries." (Florida)
- "Many thanks for sending me *God's Joy Regardless of Circumstances*. This book has been a real stream in the desert that I have been able to drink from. I have been blessed tremendously by this book. My life has not been the same since I started reading it.

I have used this book to help many people on my radio programme every Sunday. Many people have given their lives to Christ because of these messages." (Zambia)

- "Only this year I faced a lot of challenges. As a result I became bitter at heart. The wonderful Scripture verses in *God's Joy Regardless of Circumstances* took away my bitterness. I am happy now. This book has instructed me how to handle any situation with God's joy. I now can see God's solution to my life challenges by the presence of God's joy inside me. Your God-given insight has given new meaning to my spiritual life. Thank you for the encouragement through your writings." (Lome-Togo West Africa)

God's Wisdom Is Available to You

- "I did not sleep last night after reading your book *God's Wisdom is Available to You.* Thank you for your wonderful work. Because of persecution against my ministry, I spent a considerable amount of time in the hospital because of depression. I am now well and healthy in Jesus' name. Thank you for your help. I will be teaching members of my church from key text in your book. Please be my mentor, teacher and counselor." (Ghana)

- "I thank God each and every day for Jack and Judy Hartman. When I started reading your book on wisdom, everything was going wrong in my life. This book revived my spirit and my faith in God. It has changed my life. The Bible used to be like Greek to me. Now I can read it and understand it. I can't put this book down because I know I need to absorb it. I'm going through it for a second time. This book is one of the best things that has ever happened to me. I thank you both and I thank God." (Florida)

- "You did a fantastic job on this book. It is an encyclopedia on God's wisdom. The writing style is just great. Many books don't bring the reader through the subject the way this book does. I'm very impressed with that. You have made it a real joy for me to study and re-digest Scripture. This book has been very good for me." (North Carolina)

A Close and Intimate Relationship with God

- "Your book, *A Close and Intimate Relationship with God*, is tremendous. I thought that I had a close relationship with God, but this book really opened my eyes. I now can see many things that I still need to do to be even closer to God. I couldn't put this book down. When I had to stop reading, I couldn't wait to get back to it the next day. Every chapter is filled with Scripture that is very helpful to me. I will be making many changes in my life as a result of reading this awesome book. Thank you and God bless you." (New Hampshire)

- "Thank you for giving me a copy of your book *A Close and Intimate Relationship with God*. This book is written so clearly that all instructions are to the point. My life has been greatly changed and refreshed. The presence of God has become very strong in my life. I am at peace trusting my God to meet every need. My mind is totally on God. I can clearly hear His voice. I am receiving guidance and direction from Him as a result of this book. I cannot afford to spend a day without reading this book. I carry it with me wherever I go." (Zambia)

- "Thank you for your book titled *A Close and Intimate Relationship with God*. This inspiring book helped me to draw closer to our heavenly Father. In Chapter 25 you said that Paul and Silas were praising God in prison. I was having a challenging day when I read this chapter. God spoke through your book to praise Him no matter what circumstances I faced. Thank you for that inspiration. The information on dying to self in the last chapter where Paul said that he dies daily really encouraged me. I am learning to do much better putting God first, others second and myself last. Thank you at Lamplight Ministries for the thousands of people around the world that you are supporting. May the dear Lord bless you abundantly." (China)

Unshakable Faith in Almighty God

- "I thank God for the book *Unshakable Faith in Almighty God*. Because I am not indigenous Chinese, it is not easy to fellowship with the local Chinese. When I got this book I was able to see a way in the wilderness. It became my guide and light every day. When I was just about to give up Christianity, God at the right time provided this book to me. The truths and clear instruction in this book are direct from the throne of God. I am determined to move on with God come what may. I praise God that is He able to raise people we have never seen like Jack and Judy Hartman to speak into our lives through their publications. God bless the Hartman family. One day when Christ comes it will be exciting for them to see how they have influenced the world for God in Jesus' name. I am so grateful for these free books that cost a lot of money in publishing, printing and postage." (China)

- "I have been pastoring in Belgium for the past 15 years. In the past our church was flourishing and doing very well until late last year when my praise and worship leader decided to break away and form another church. This was a very big blow to us as a church. Most of our strong and committed members left the church with some of the church instruments. My wife almost gave up. She was discouraged. This also affected our finances. Pastor Jim gave me a book titled *Unshakable Faith in Almighty God*. Before I read this book my faith was shaken and I almost gave up. This book took me step by step to show me how to make my faith grow. You cannot read this book and remain the same. I have been using the book to preach to the few members that remain with us. In the past four months we have experienced revival. The anointing is so strong and the members have been strengthened so much through the preaching from this book. We are determined to not give up. God bless the Hartmans for being a blessing to us in Europe." (Belgium)

- "*Unshakable Faith in Almighty God* has amazed me. The language is so simple and very clear to understand. This book is powerful and life-changing. I will always hang on to this book. Brother Hartman, God's favour and wisdom are so great on your life. I believe this book is written on very heavy anointing from God. Your reward in heaven will be so great. All those who have sown seeds in your ministry should rejoice. When I wake up, I read this book. Before going to bed, I read it. I will continue to go through it again and again. Your ministry is a big blessing to me. You are always in our prayers." (Zambia)

How to Study the Bible

- "Your book, *How to Study the Bible*, is a gem. Since I became a Christian 41 years ago, I have studied the Bible using a variety of methods. Your method is simple and straightforward. It involves hard work, but the rewards are real. I have read several of your books and this book is the one I would highly recommend to any Christian because this book is the foundation. God bless you, brother." (England)
- "My wife and I are utilizing the Bible study method that you explained in *How to Study the Bible*. We are really growing spiritually as a result. Our old methods of study were not nearly as fruitful. Thank you for writing about your method." (Idaho)
- "I have read almost all of your books and they are outstanding. The one that blessed me the most was *How to Study the Bible*. The study part was excellent, but the meditation chapters were very, very beneficial. I am indebted to you for sharing these. I purchased 30 copies to give to friends. Every earnest student of God's Word needs a copy." (Tennessee)

Increased Energy and Vitality

- "It is so great to meet Christians on the same wave length. In your book *Increased Energy and Vitality*, you are writing almost word for word in some cases what I have been saying to patients for almost 30 years." (Ohio)

- "Last year I obtained a copy of your book *Increased Energy and Vitality*. My wife and I have read and have in fact changed our ways of eating and drinking and exercising because of your influence. We thoroughly appreciate this God-centered message that is so well presented. I have enclosed an order for more of these books. We know many people we wish to help. This is the first step in spreading the news you have so generously put together. Thank you for your efforts. May God continue your leadership in writing, speaking and guidance." (Illinois)

- "I have benefited tremendously from reading and personally applying the principles learned from your book *Increased Energy and Vitality*. By applying your methods, I have gained additional energy especially during my low periods from 2:00 p.m. to 4:00 p.m. I highly recommend your book to others. Keep up the good work." (Florida)

100 Years from Today

- "*100 Years From Today* told me that going to church and doing good deeds won't get me to heaven. I believe in Jesus Christ. I believe He died for our sins and that He forgives us for what we did wrong. Heaven is where I belong. I am born again. I have a new life. This book has changed my life." (Florida)

- "I am writing to express my deep and profound appreciation for your book *100 Years from Today*.

I recently began attending a Bible-based church where I found a copy of this book in their lending library. I read the book in one sitting, reading the words aloud to myself. Your book explained details from the Bible that I had not learned before. I thank you for taking the time and effort to write this book. My written words can never fully express how grateful I am to you. By my actions, a changed life and a deep sense of peace, I hope to bear fruit by helping others." (Massachusetts)

- "I find it hard to put *100 Years from Today* down. I read the whole book in a day and a half. I never knew how much pain and suffering Jesus went through to pay for my sins. I learned how much He loves us." (Florida)

Nuggets of Faith

- "Your books, tapes and meditation cards are really a blessing to me. They came at just the right time. I am preparing sermons on faith from *Nuggets of Faith*. I want the congregation to be constantly learning God's Word in order to have much more faith. I also have been encouraged personally through that book. It is awesome. Thank you for your powerful and inspiring publications." (Zambia)
- "We give *Nuggets of Faith* to people who are hospitalized, for birthdays, to saved and unsaved. Everyone who has received one tells us 'It's the best little book I've ever read. It's so clear and easy to understand.'" (Indiana)
- "I work as a store manager. Today I was told that I was no longer needed. Praise Jesus that only two

months prior to this date I had accepted the Lord Jesus as my personal Lord and Savior. I have faith that the Lord was working to bring me to a new direction. I am writing to thank you for your excellent book *Nuggets of Faith*. The moment I arrived home after having been dismissed, I received this book in the mail. I completed this short but awesome book in a little over two hours. It has helped my faith to grow stronger and I know that I will begin a great new journey tomorrow. God bless you." (New York)

Comments on our Scripture Meditation Cards

- "My back was hurting so badly that I couldn't get comfortable. I was miserable whether I sat or stood or laid down. I didn't know what to do. Suddenly I thought of the Scripture cards on healing that my husband had purchased. I decided to meditate on the Scripture in these cards. I was only on the second card when, all of a sudden, I felt heat go from my neck down through my body. The Lord had healed me. I never knew it could happen so fast. The pain has not come back." (Idaho)

- "My wife and I use your Scripture cards every day when we pray. I read the card for that day in English and then my wife repeats it in Norwegian. We then pray based upon the Scripture reference on that day's card. These cards have been very beneficial to us. We would like to see the Scripture cards published in the Norwegian language." (Norway)

- "Your Scripture cards have been very helpful to my wife and myself. We have taped them to the walls in our home and we meditate on them constantly. I also take four or five cards with me every day when I go to work. I meditate on them while I drive. The Scripture on these cards is a constant source of encouragement to us. We ask for permission to translate *Trust God for Your Finances*. This book is badly needed by the people in Turkey." (This permission was granted.) (Turkey)

- "My mom is 95 years old. She was in the Bergen-Belsen Concentration Camp in Germany from 1943 to 1945. She has always had a lot of worry and fear. My mother was helped greatly in overcoming this problem by your Scripture cards titled *Freedom from Worry and Fear*. She was helped so much that she asked me to order another set to give to a friend." (California)

- "I am overwhelmed about the revelations in your Scripture Meditation Cards. These Scripture cards have helped me so much that I cannot write enough on this sheet of paper. We have gone through a five-day programme in our church using the Scripture cards. My faith has increased tremendously. I no longer am submitting to my own will and desires, but I am now submitting to the will of God and it is so fantastic. God bless you, Jack and Judy Hartman." (Ghana)

- "I am very enthusiastic about your Scripture cards and your tape titled *Receive Healing from the Lord*. I love your tape. The clarity of your voice and your sincerity and compassion will encourage sick people. They can listen to this tape throughout the day, before they go to sleep at night, while they are driving to the doctor's office, in the hospital, etc. The tape is filled with Scripture and many good comments on Scripture. This cassette tape and your Scripture cards on healing are powerful tools that will help many sick people." (Tennessee) (NOTE:

The ten cassette tapes for our Scripture Meditation Cards are available on 60-minute CDs as well.)

- "I meditate constantly on the healing cards and listen to your tape on healing over and over. Your voice is so soothing. You are a wonderful teacher. My faith is increasing constantly." (New Hampshire).
- "I thank God for you. I carry your Scripture Meditation Cards in my purse. The Scriptures you have chosen are all powerful. What a blessing to be able to meditate on the Word of God at any time, anywhere. Thank you for your hard work. The Scripture cards are a blessing to me." (Canada)

We offer you a substantial quantity discount

From the beginning of our ministry we have been led of the Lord to offer the same quantity discount to individuals that we offer to Christian bookstores. Each individual has a sphere of influence with a specific group of people. We believe that you know many people who need to learn the scriptural contents of our publications.

The Word of God encourages us to give freely to others. We encourage you to give selected copies of these publications to people you know who need help in the specific areas that are covered by our publications. See our order form for specific information on the quantity discounts that we make available to you so that you can share our books, Scripture Meditation Cards and CDs with others.

A request to our readers

If this book has helped you, we would like to receive your comments so that we can share them with others. Your comments can encourage other people to study our publications to learn from the scriptural contents of these publications.

When we receive a letter containing comments on any of our books, cassette tapes or Scripture Meditation Cards, we prayerfully take out excerpts from these letters. These selected excerpts are included in our newsletters and occasionally in our advertising and promotional materials.

If any of our publications have been a blessing to you, please share your comments with us so that we can share them with others. Tell us in your own words what a specific publication has meant to you and why you would recommend it to others. Please give as much specific information as possible. We prefer three or four paragraphs so that we can condense this into one paragraph.

Thank you for taking a few minutes of your time to encourage other people to learn from the scripture references in our publications.

ORDER FORM FOR BOOKS

Book Title	Quantity	Total
What Does God Say? ($18)	_____ x $18 =	_____
Live Continually in the Presence of God ($14)	_____ x $14 =	_____
Glorious Eternal Life in Heaven ($14)	_____ x $14 =	_____
Reverent Awe of God ($14)	_____ x $14 =	_____
God's Plan for Your Life ($14)	_____ x $14 =	_____
You Can Hear the Voice of God ($14)	_____ x $14 =	_____
God's Instructions for Growing Older ($14)	_____ x $14 =	_____
Effective Prayer ($14)	_____ x $14 =	_____
Overcoming Fear ($14)	_____ x $14 =	_____
A Close and Intimate Relationship with God ($14)	_____ x $14 =	_____
God's Joy Regardless of Circumstances ($14)	_____ x $14 =	_____
Victory Over Adversity ($14)	_____ x $14 =	_____
Receive Healing from the Lord ($14)	_____ x $14 =	_____
Unshakable Faith in Almighty God ($14)	_____ x $14 =	_____
Exchange Your Worries for God's Perfect Peace ($14)	_____ x $14 =	_____
God's Wisdom is Available to You ($14)	_____ x $14 =	_____
Quiet Confidence in the Lord ($14)	_____ x $14 =	_____
Never, Never Give Up ($14)	_____ x $14 =	_____
Increased Energy and Vitality ($14)	_____ x $14 =	_____
Trust God For Your Finances ($14)	_____ x $14 =	_____
How to Study the Bible ($10)	_____ x $10 =	_____
Nuggets of Faith ($10)	_____ x $10 =	_____
100 Years From Today ($10)	_____ x $10 =	_____

    Price of books _____

    Minus 40% discount for 5-9 books _____

    Minus 50% discount for 10 or more books _____

    Net price of order _____

    Add 15% **before discount** for shipping and handling _____

    Florida residents only, add 7% sales tax _____

    Tax deductible contribution to Lamplight Ministries, Inc. _____

Enclosed check or money order (do not send cash) _____

(Foreign orders must be submitted in U.S. dollars.)

Please make check payable to **Lamplight Ministries, Inc**. and mail to:
PO Box 1307, Dunedin, FL 34697

MC____ Visa____ AmEx____ Disc.____ Card # _____

Exp Date _____ 3-digit code _____ Signature _____

Name _____

Address _____

City _____ Phone _____

State or Province _____ Zip or Postal Code _____

Email _____ Website: _____

ORDER FORM FOR BOOKS

Book Title	Quantity	Total
What Does God Say? ($18)	_____ x $18 =	_____
Live Continually in the Presence of God ($14)	_____ x $14 =	_____
Glorious Eternal Life in Heaven ($14)	_____ x $14 =	_____
Reverent Awe of God ($14)	_____ x $14 =	_____
God's Plan for Your Life ($14)	_____ x $14 =	_____
You Can Hear the Voice of God ($14)	_____ x $14 =	_____
God's Instructions for Growing Older ($14)	_____ x $14 =	_____
Effective Prayer ($14)	_____ x $14 =	_____
Overcoming Fear ($14)	_____ x $14 =	_____
A Close and Intimate Relationship with God ($14)	_____ x $14 =	_____
God's Joy Regardless of Circumstances ($14)	_____ x $14 =	_____
Victory Over Adversity ($14)	_____ x $14 =	_____
Receive Healing from the Lord ($14)	_____ x $14 =	_____
Unshakable Faith in Almighty God ($14)	_____ x $14 =	_____
Exchange Your Worries for God's Perfect Peace ($14)	_____ x $14 =	_____
God's Wisdom is Available to You ($14)	_____ x $14 =	_____
Quiet Confidence in the Lord ($14)	_____ x $14 =	_____
Never, Never Give Up ($14)	_____ x $14 =	_____
Increased Energy and Vitality ($14)	_____ x $14 =	_____
Trust God For Your Finances ($14)	_____ x $14 =	_____
How to Study the Bible ($10)	_____ x $10 =	_____
Nuggets of Faith ($10)	_____ x $10 =	_____
100 Years From Today ($10)	_____ x $10 =	_____

    Price of books _____

    Minus 40% discount for 5-9 books _____

    Minus 50% discount for 10 or more books _____

    Net price of order _____

    Add 15% **before discount** for shipping and handling _____

    Florida residents only, add 7% sales tax _____

    Tax deductible contribution to Lamplight Ministries, Inc. _____

Enclosed check or money order (do not send cash) _____

(Foreign orders must be submitted in U.S. dollars.)

Please make check payable to **Lamplight Ministries, Inc.** and mail to:
PO Box 1307, Dunedin, FL 34697

MC____ Visa____ AmEx____ Disc.____ Card # _____

Exp Date _____ 3-digit code _____ Signature _____

Name _____

Address _____

City _____ Phone _____

State or Province _____ Zip or Postal Code _____

Email _____ Website: _____

ORDER FORM FOR SCRIPTURE MEDITATION CARDS AND CDs

SCRIPTURE MEDITATION CARDS	QUANTITY	PRICE
A Closer Relationship with the Lord ($5)	_____	_____
Continually Increasing Faith in God ($5)	_____	_____
Enjoy God's Wonderful Peace ($5)	_____	_____
Financial Instructions from God ($5)	_____	_____
Find God's Will for Your Life ($5)	_____	_____
Freedom from Worry and Fear ($5)	_____	_____
God is Always with You ($5)	_____	_____
Our Father's Wonderful Love ($5)	_____	_____
Receive God's Blessing in Adversity ($5)	_____	_____
Receive Healing from the Lord ($5)	_____	_____

CDs	QUANTITY	PRICE
A Closer Relationship with the Lord ($10)	_____	_____
Continually Increasing Faith in God ($10)	_____	_____
Enjoy God's Wonderful Peace ($10)	_____	_____
Financial Instructions from God ($10)	_____	_____
Find God's Will for Your Life ($10)	_____	_____
Freedom from Worry and Fear ($10)	_____	_____
God is Always with You ($10)	_____	_____
Our Father's Wonderful Love ($10)	_____	_____
Receive God's Blessing in Adversity ($10)	_____	_____
Receive Healing from the Lord ($10)	_____	_____

TOTAL PRICE _____

Minus 40% discount for 5-9 Scripture Cards and CDs _____
Minus 50% discount for 10 or more Scripture Cards and CDs _____
Net price of order _____
Add 15% **before discount** for shipping and handling _____
Florida residents only, add 7% sales tax _____
Tax deductible contribution to Lamplight Ministries, Inc. _____
Enclosed check or money order (do not send cash) _____
(Foreign orders must be submitted in U.S. dollars.)

Please make check payable to **Lamplight Ministries, Inc**. and mail to:
PO Box 1307, Dunedin, FL 34697

MC____ Visa____ AmEx____ Disc.____ Card # _____

Exp Date _____ 3-digit code _____ Signature _____

Name _____

Address _____

City _____ Phone _____

State or Province _____ Zip or Postal Code _____

Email _____ Website: _____

ORDER FORM FOR SCRIPTURE MEDITATION CARDS AND CDs

SCRIPTURE MEDITATION CARDS	QUANTITY	PRICE
A Closer Relationship with the Lord ($5)		
Continually Increasing Faith in God ($5)		
Enjoy God's Wonderful Peace ($5)		
Financial Instructions from God ($5)		
Find God's Will for Your Life ($5)		
Freedom from Worry and Fear ($5)		
God is Always with You ($5)		
Our Father's Wonderful Love ($5)		
Receive God's Blessing in Adversity ($5)		
Receive Healing from the Lord ($5)		

CDs	QUANTITY	PRICE
A Closer Relationship with the Lord ($10)		
Continually Increasing Faith in God ($10)		
Enjoy God's Wonderful Peace ($10)		
Financial Instructions from God ($10)		
Find God's Will for Your Life ($10)		
Freedom from Worry and Fear ($10)		
God is Always with You ($10)		
Our Father's Wonderful Love ($10)		
Receive God's Blessing in Adversity ($10)		
Receive Healing from the Lord ($10)		

TOTAL PRICE _____

Minus 40% discount for 5-9 Scripture Cards and CDs _____
Minus 50% discount for 10 or more Scripture Cards and CDs _____
Net price of order _____
Add 15% ***before discount*** for shipping and handling _____
Florida residents only, add 7% sales tax _____
Tax deductible contribution to Lamplight Ministries, Inc. _____
Enclosed check or money order (do not send cash) _____
(Foreign orders must be submitted in U.S. dollars.)

Please make check payable to **Lamplight Ministries, Inc.** and mail to:
PO Box 1307, Dunedin, FL 34697

MC____ Visa____ AmEx____ Disc.____ Card # _____

Exp Date _____ 3-digit code _____ Signature _____

Name _____

Address _____

City _____ Phone _____

State or Province _____ Zip or Postal Code _____

Email _____ Website: _____

www.ingramcontent.com/pod-product-compliance
Lightning Source LLC
LaVergne TN
LVHW051125080426
835510LV00018B/2236